being

Green

a COLORFUL JOURNEY

HOWARD GREEN

PAGE PUBLISHING, INC.
New York, NY

First originally published by Page Publishing, Inc. 2017

ISBN 978-1-68409-525-4 (Paperback)
ISBN 978-1-68409-697-8 (Hard Cover)
ISBN 978-1-68409-526-1 (Digital)

Printed in the United States of America

Dedicated to all the struggling children in the world.

Introduction

This is my story. I was brought up in the Bronx by an insane woman who was in and out of mental institutions during my formative years. My dad was physically and verbally abusive, and my brother was hardly ever around. I realized, at an early age, that I was different, and it was not easy for this budding gay boy to be growing up at a time when there were no role models, and the way people spoke of gays left me feeling like something akin to a murderer.

At twenty-one years of age, I married a woman, and we were happily married for seven years. However, my early upbringing left me scarred and scared, and for the longest time, I fled from one job to another. In need of a temporary refuge, I volunteered myself into a mental hospital for thirty days.

Things finally began to look up when I obtained a job as a secretary at 20th Century-Fox Film Corporation.

I went quickly from secretary to publicist and had many rewarding experiences working with the likes of Clint Eastwood, Jack Lemmon, Lucille Ball, John Denver, and Johnny Mathis and developed a friendship with my life-long obsession, singer-actress Doris Day.

Battling my insecurities and fears was not easy, but I persevered, saw a few analysts along the way, meditated, and have turned my life around. For anyone who feels that there is no light at the end of the tunnel, I believe my life-time struggles may prove to be an inspiration.

Chapter 1

MIXED EMOTIONS

I never knew my mother as a sane woman. She had two nervous breakdowns before I was born, and unfortunately, she bore the scars throughout her life.

I was born August 30, 1942, on Pelham Parkway, the Bronx, New York. Back then, neighborhoods were real neighborly. Everyone knew everybody else's business, and kids had no rigid schedules apart from school. We played in the streets until dark, and parents didn't worry about kidnappings, rape, and the other atrocities likened to this day and age. In general, most kids just played outside and had a great time. Most kids, not me. My childhood was far from great.

My earliest memory is of Mom being taken away to a mental hospital when I was five years old. I cried hysterically, and since my dad and his cousin Sam fooled my mother into thinking they were just going for "a nice little walk," I harbored ill feelings toward him from that day forth.

I loved my mother dearly. Underneath all her turmoil, it was easy to see that she had a heart of gold, and despite her condition, I never doubted her love for me. She was away for a year, and when she returned, I was one happy kid. Having been "treated" with shock therapy and icy baths, she had scars that seemed to go even deeper than before. Even at five, I could sense what she was going through. It didn't take long to realize that if you pushed the wrong button, she would be off on a tangent somewhere in fantasy land.

I was a sensitive child, and I felt very sorry for her, especially during her outbursts, which happened with regularity. For example, the doorbell would ring, and my mom would grab me. "Don't answer it!" she would cry. "There are Communists out there with a bomb." My brother, Phil, nine years older than me, was usually nowhere to be seen. I can't really blame him for leaving that atmosphere whenever possible. As for Dad, he only made matters worse. He demeaned my mom at every turn, and I felt extreme empathy for her and just as extreme resentment toward him. His relationship with me was no better. He abused me both mentally and physically. "You'll never get anywhere in life!" "Why can't you be like so-and-so?" and "You're a dummy!" were just a few examples of his parenting skills. His physical abuse came to me not in a sexual sense but by beating me with his trusty strap, buckle side up. All of this, especially Dad's treatment of Mom, has made me as sympathetic as I am today. I feel deeply for those who are troubled.

Babies typically stop using pacifiers on their own between the ages of two and four. I was so frightened and mentally screwed up that I needed pacifying until the age of fifteen or so. Instead of the typical pacifier, I sucked my fingers and hid my face behind my pillow. I carried that pillow with me all around the house. If I was watching television in the foyer, and the doorbell rang, I would quickly discard the pillow by throwing it on the couch in the next room. I felt ashamed of my habit, but it took me a long time to get over it.

On top of it all, Dad was an inveterate gambler. Most nights, he would leave for the "club.'" He would meet his cronies there, and they would play cards and discuss the horse races to their hearts' delight. I never ventured into the club; if Dad was an example of the membership, I wanted nothing to do with it. To this day, gambling holds little appeal for me. I love Las Vegas, but I don't gamble too much.

Not to say that all was bad all the time. My aunt Joan, uncle Irving, and cousin Paul lived a few blocks away, and Paul, who was close to my age, was my first real friend. We would spend hours at the neighborhood playground, on the monkey bars, slides, seesaws, and swings. Those were times I cherish! Sadly, they moved to California when I was five, and to this day, I can still see their car heading westward. It was a very sad moment for me, and I cried hysterically.

My grandmother, Bessie Rappaport, lived on Tremont Avenue, which wasn't close, but Mom would visit her often, usually dragging me along. Granny was a nice woman, but she had wet kisses, and I tried every which way to avoid the dreaded attack of her lips. Additionally, her house couldn't have been very clean because it was infested with roaches. She meant well and always offered me lunch, but when you find roaches crawling around your plate, the thought of eating is the furthest thing from your mind.

Grandma lived with her old-maid daughter, my aunt Julia, who wasn't a very nice lady. She couldn't stand my father, and the feeling was mutual. She never came to my house unless Dad was out. If he came home when she was inside, she would take off like a shot! Julia tried to turn me against my dad. Not that I needed any coaxing, but it wasn't her place, and I resented her for it. She was deservedly lonely, but one afternoon, I discovered that she was more than that when she and I were alone in the house. I was scratching myself where the sun doesn't shine, and upon noticing that, she motioned for me to come over. "Come to Auntie. Have you got an itch? Let Auntie see." Well, I may have been a kid, but I knew something was wrong there, so I changed the subject as quickly as I could.

I guess music was my earliest escape. I recall singing along with Betty Hutton to the strains of "Doctor, Lawyer, Indian Chief," with Judy Garland singing "Look for the Silver Lining," and with Danny Kaye in his great rendition of "Ballin' the Jack." How I loved singing along and making up dance steps. And at that time, I discovered that I had a pretty nice singing voice. I also loved the movies, particularly the musicals. Betty Grable was an early favorite, and I developed a strong crush on her. Chances are, I was the only five-year-old to have that famous World War II pinup of Grable pasted on my headboard.

Like many affairs of the heart, that one was destined to end, especially when I discovered Doris Day. Those early musical films of hers took me somewhere I needed to be, away from the dark reality of my home life. I loved her beautiful singing voice, and that gorgeous, warm smile of hers was just what the doctor ordered. She was my friend, and I couldn't get enough. Every month, I would wait expectantly for the new movie magazines to come out. As I rifled through the magazine racks, I would look from side to side to make sure none of the neighborhood guys would see me. Movie magazines? Much too girly for them! But not for me! I'd save every photo of Doris I could get my hands on, and I kept a scrapbook filled with her pictures. I've obsessed over Doris Day from my earliest days to the present time. We'll get into that later. Another family tragedy awaited.

My mom was getting worse by the day, and in 1950, she was carted off once again to a mental hospital. By that time, I was getting bashed on all sides. Between my dad's abuses, the fun the neighborhood kids made about Mom, and my rapidly spiraling weight, I was not a happy camper.

In kindergarten, I was chosen to appear in a school musical. I was cast as a baker (I'm sure my chubbiness helped land me that role). "Hot cross buns, hot cross buns, one a penny, two a penny, hot cross buns." That was the extent of my part. The music director boosted my spirits considerably when she called me her little treasure. That was it. A compliment! I don't think I'd ever had one before. I was floating. At that very moment, I decided to become an actor/singer. But that dream was not to be fulfilled.

When I was eight or so, it became clear to me that I just didn't fit in with the other guys. I didn't like sports. I enjoyed movie musicals, and I felt more comfortable playing with the neighborhood girls. When the guys chose up sides for baseball, I was always the last one to be picked. I felt great shame over that, and so I gravitated to the girls where I felt safe.

Now, let's see. I loved playing with girls, liked to sing and dance. Aha! There was something most definitely queer about all that! At that point, I felt like I was constantly masquerading, never revealing my true self. I was ashamed of being me, and I thought my manner of speech would only call attention to my difference. My speech was actually fine, but all I knew about gays was the stereotype of a swishy, lisping queen prancing about with his hair on fire. I assumed that was how I came across, but that was not reality. I did enjoy playing with the guys when they played games like Johnny on the Pony (I could play that once today and wind up in the emergency room!) and ring-a-levio, but I always felt like an outcast—a feeling which I would harbor for many years to come.

After graduating from PS 105 to PS 83, I made a new discovery: I *did* like girls. I may have led a gay lifestyle for most of my adult life, but I think, like most, I'm just a sexual being. Labels are for soup cans! Not for me! I had a mad crush on Ellen Zisholtz, a dark, extremely intelligent beauty. I remember going to her house after school, meeting her family, and feeling great while there. I bought her an ankle bracelet, and she wore it with pride until Jack Hammer arrived on the scene. He was tall, dark, handsome, and very popular. He flashed his eyes on my Ellen, and next thing I knew, he too had bought her an ankle bracelet. Oh, how I suffered. Being the meek one in this scenario, I gave up easily, and that was the end of my first romance.

A highlight of my days at PS 83 was being cast as the captain in our school production of the Gilbert and Sullivan musical *HMS Pinafore*. I sang; I danced. I was in my element! Heaven! I was only at that school for a year since we were switched to the brand-new junior high school 135 the following term.

I turned thirteen, a time when every nice little Jewish boy became bar mitzvah-ed. I studied hard and learned my lessons well, but it really was a sad affair. Mother was always denying that we were Jewish. "I believe in Jesus Christ," she would cry out, and I had to hide my bar mitzvah plans from her. So one school-day morning, Dad and I snuck off to a local temple. I said my prayers, and off I went to school. No celebration like my friends had. No nothing. I didn't even tell my classmates. What should have been a joyous occasion only left me feeling cheated and empty.

I was only 5'5" at the time, but by the age of thirteen, I weighed 195 pounds and had a thirty-nine-and-one-half-inch waist. I couldn't find love at home or feel accepted by the neighborhood kids, so I'm sure my overeating served as a great source of comfort. But after much bullying, I dieted, and I meant business. After three months, I lost sixty pounds, and I loved the attention I was getting from the neighborhood kids. I vowed never to get fat again, and to this day, I get on the scale first thing each morning.

At the age of fourteen, I had my sights set on attending the School of Performing Arts (on which the movie *Fame* was based). But unfortunately, my low self-esteem got the better of me. I applied, but just before auditions began, I developed a bad cold. Mind over matter, I'm sure. I was afraid of failure, and that was the bottom line.

And so I attended Christopher Columbus High School. I wasn't a great student, but I was chosen for a great role in *My Fair Lady*, and that was my happiest high school memory, hands down. I played Alfred P. Doolittle, the always-drunk father of Eliza Doolittle. Again, I was singing and dancing. Our director, Mr. Van Reil, came running to me after one of our many rehearsals. He told me that a showbiz friend of his watched the rehearsal and told him that I was good enough to play the part on Broadway. I was thrilled. Van Reil went so far as to come to my home, where he tried to convince my parents to encourage me to take show business seriously. But there was no convincing them. They never encouraged me in any way about anything. Why should this be any different?

I joined the glee club, and that was another high point in my high school years. I've always loved to sing. In fact, when I'm not singing, I've usually got a song rolling around in my head. I developed that habit early in life. It made me feel good then, and it has stuck.

There may have been a few high points, but by the age of fifteen, my mental state was in a shambles. The combination of Dad's verbal assaults and beatings, plus Mom's state of mind, plus the bullying tossed my way had really taken its toll on me. There were times, in fact, when I just couldn't leave the house. I feared running into neighborhood kids, and thought that if I did, I'd have to say hello and give myself, my gay self away. I had to do something, and so I walked two miles to Jacobi hospital in the hopes that someone, anyone, could help me lighten my load. I asked to see a counselor, and in a short time, found myself seated in the office of a young doctor. He listened intently as I told him my life story with an emphasis on my sexual identity. His answer? "It's just a phase you're going through, and I'm sure you'll get over it." Geez! I walked home, feeling hopelessly distraught and feeling that the doctor just didn't know what he was talking about.

My psychological leanings may have bent toward the gay side, but how I admired beautiful women! There was one gal in class who looked very much like actress Elizabeth Taylor. I couldn't take my eyes off her, and she knew it. Nothing ventured, nothing gained. I never spoke to the girl. I did make friends with a couple of kids in school, but if it's true that you're judged by the company you keep, we were all a bunch of losers.

During better days, I hung out with a popular group of guys called the Barnes Boys, named after Barnes Avenue, the street where they lived. Two exceptions were me and Harris "Heshy" Gold. He and I lived at 2160 Wallace Avenue. I did make some good friends there. Mel Citrin is a friend to this day. Mel, a wonderful dancer, taught me to dance to the strains of Elvis Presley hits and other popular songs of the mid-'50s. Like all things musical, I took well to dancing. In fact, I won a number of dance competitions. My partner, Sandy Kalikstein, and I appeared a few times on a local New York TV show called *Alan Freed's Rock 'n' Roll Dance Party,* and that's where I won a Lindy hop contest with a sterling silver tea set as the prize. I promptly turned it over to Mom, and she loved it. Anything I could do to make her happy made me happy too.

Chapter 2

LOVE AND MARRIAGE

I n 1957, Heshy and I tried to get into *The Tonight Show*. We had no advance tickets, so we waited on a long line of people hoping to acquire seats. Shortly after our arrival, along comes actress Betty Hutton, dressed to the nines and, most obviously, three sheets to the wind! She looked at our group, inquired about us, and then proceeded to plop down on the floor and tell the production people, "I'm not going in unless my friends can come up and see the show!" Then the elevator door opened. She motioned for me and Heshy to follow her, and naturally, we did. Then she whispered, "Remember, you're my relatives from Battle Creek, Michigan." Some staffers proceeded to lead her to the green room and led us right out the door!

In my mid to late teens, I dated now and then, just so the neighborhood guys could see what a "man" I was. I even went so far as to intentionally date a girl with a bad reputation. I took her to the movies, walked her home, and filled with expectation, I kissed her. But I felt nothing! I'm pretty sure the feeling was mutual. We said our hasty good nights, and that was that. My virginity remained intact, and we never spoke to each other again.

My high school grades were slightly above average, and since my parents couldn't afford to get me into a better school, I was accepted by Bronx Community College. As it turned out, the soundtrack recording of Doris Day's latest musical film, *Billy Rose's Jumbo*, was released on the very first day of school. Still over the top over Doris Day, I bought the double album (first things first!) and then headed for class. At the school's front entrance, I observed happy kids cheerily chatting away. Once again, I felt like an outsider. Now I had a choice: scary kids at college or my old friend Doris? I quickly turned and headed for home, and that was the beginning and end of my college career. I never did go back.

Now I needed a job. It didn't take long to find employment as a bank clerk at Manufacturers Hanover Trust Co. on Fifty-Seventh Street and Lexington Avenue. I enjoyed the work and made a couple of work friends. However, it was the start of my inexplicable fear of coworkers who, it seemed to me, were seeing right through me, the homosexual me! The loser! That kind of thinking became a pattern that was to hound me for quite some time.

The high point during that period was meeting Doris Day for the first time. It was 1960, and her film *Midnight Lace* was opening at Radio City Music Hall. Thanks to a photo in the *New York Daily News* of her arriving at Grand Central Station, I set out to see my silver-screen goddess. Somehow, I mustered up the nerve to call Universal Pictures, talk like I knew what I was talking about, and told the girl in publicity that I was a reporter for *Elle,* a popular French magazine. To my utter astonishment, she told me that there would be a foreign press conference at the Plaza Hotel the next day, but she cautioned, my name wasn't on their list, so I couldn't attend. Well, that wasn't about to stop me. I was determined.

As it turned out, that was the day her *Life* magazine cover came out with the headline, "Sunny Doris Day in a Shivery Role." I picked it up and had it tucked neatly under my arm as I waited on the hotel floor where the conference was to be held. My back was turned when I heard that familiar voice of hers. I turned around, and sure enough, there she was, coming down the aisle with two guys from the staff at Universal. I was shivering in my shoes as I held out the magazine and said, "Ms. Day, would you please sign this for me?" She gave me that dazzling smile of hers, the smile that had been warming my heart for years, and said, "Of course." Then she proceeded to go into the banquet hall. I left the hotel, floating on air.

After a long stretch of going nowhere on the job, I sought out new employment. I called in sick and took off for the city. But my mother, bless her heart, called the bank manager and squealed on me. Believe it or not, he was so impressed by her honesty that he gave me a promotion. Go figure! I was transferred to a branch at Fifty-Seventh and Fifth Avenue as a teller, and I really enjoyed being there. There I was, in the heart of the big city, and it was quite a thrill for this yokel from the Bronx.

Many celebrities came to the branch, and star-struck little me was in heaven. Sidney Poitier was a regular, and he always came to my window. However, he scared me. Such an imposing presence, and at the time, he was one of the biggest stars in Hollywood. Martin Sheen came in quite frequently with his agent, and in the mid-'60s, his attractive appearance reminded me of the late James Dean. Zsa Zsa Gabor was another regular, and she always made a regal entrance with her tiny white poodle clutched to her chest. Noticing how the customers were ogling her, she turned to them with a wave that would have done Queen Elizabeth

proud and cried out, "Hello, dahlings!" Famed ice skater
Dick Button was another customer, and he was a sweet,
unassuming man who regularly stopped at my window.

That summer, I was invited to join my friend,
Marvin Watsky, and his family at a local beach club called
Shorehaven. While there, we met the Moss family, and
Marvin and I hung out with Helene, their eldest daughter, who was just a few years younger than myself. She was
attractive in a Cher Bono sort of way—thin but shapely
with beautiful dark brown eyes and a shy but charming way
about her. As we rode home in the Watsky car, I noticed the
Moss family car directly in front of ours. Helene's mother
appeared to be coaxing her daughter to turn around and
wave at me. I found it flattering and amusing, and it turned
out to be a harbinger of very significant things to come.

Months later, Heshy invited me to join him and his
girlfriend on a double date. His girl lived in the Jerome
Avenue section of the Bronx, and I recalled that Helene
lived in that part of town. I called her, and that was the
start of our courtship. We saw a film at the Paradise Theatre
on Fordham Road, an opulent movie palace where carv-
ings and statuary lined the massive lobby, and the interior ceiling always fascinated me with its billowing clouds
slowly drifting by and stars blinking away. After the show,
we went to Krum's ice cream parlor and attacked one of

their famous hot fudge sundaes. Helene was quite shy, but there was something about her I found appealing, and so we continued to date.

As time passed, I grew fond of her, and she made it obvious to me that the feeling was mutual. But feelings of confused sexuality were still hounding me although I never took the plunge to explore them. Our dates consisted of movies and dinner, and we always ended the night with heavy petting on the couch in her apartment building lobby. We'd be there until the wee hours of the morning, and it was amusing to see her neighbors pass by, trying hard not to be obvious as they glanced our way.

Back at the bank, things were going well. I enjoyed the work, and for a change, I wasn't intimidated by any of my coworkers. But one morning I screwed up royally. We had always been told to reject any checks that weren't endorsed, and I foolishly refused to cash the check of a top-level bank executive. I thought he was testing me. But unfortunately, that wasn't the case. He walked away in a huff, and before I knew it, I was a goner.

Helene and I had been dating for nearly a year when, out of the blue, she asked me what my intentions were. There she was, a seventeen-year-old kid, and I was only twenty, and she's asking me about my intentions. I never expected that. I had no future plans in mind. But her mother had coaxed her into asking me, and I told Helene to give me some time, time to hopefully find a way out! One evening, I made up a tall tale in the hopes that it would turn Helene off. I told her that I was having the weirdest dreams, dreams about murdering people. I tried looking sinister and a bit crazed as I weaved my tale. She simply shrugged it off, and that was that. I could have just broken the relationship off, but Helene was a sensitive girl, and I was afraid she might do something rash.

In those days, the only way to leave your parents' clutches without creating a neighborhood scandal was to get married, and the thought of being away from the family loony bin was appealing, so I decided to pop the question. Since I loved the theatre, I thought the perfect evening for a proposal would be a romantic dinner followed by a great show. And what could be more romantic than a carriage ride through Central Park? We attended a revival of *Best Foot Forward* with Liza Minnelli in one of her earliest stage performances. Then we took that carriage ride, and it was there that I popped the question. As expected, Helene accepted the 1¼ carat ring I couldn't afford, and we were then officially engaged. Our engagement lasted approximately one year, and plans for the wedding were a breeze. In fact, Helene and I didn't participate at all. The details were left in the hands of her mom and dad.

Her mom was a very outgoing woman, and her dad was a terrific guy with a great sense of humor. They were fairly young, approximately early to mid-40s, and they were fun to be with. Helene's sister, Barbara, was only twelve, and she and I developed a close relationship. In fact, I'd say I had paternal feelings toward her. She always seemed to come to me for advice, and I was only too happy to help. Admittedly, one of the joys of my relationship with Helene was having a "normal" family at last. We spent many Sundays together with her folks, and I relished those fun times, especially the feeling of belonging at last.

The wedding was a grand one. There were about a hundred people I hardly knew, except for a few Bronx buddies, and to tell the truth, the entire evening felt pretty unreal. I recall the rabbi reciting Hebrew prayers as Helene and I stood at the altar. The two of us, not the least bit religious, were chuckling to one another, she behind her veil, and me trying my best to hide the smirks. At evening's end, we began our honeymoon at the Concourse Plaza Hotel, which, at the time, was the pride of the Bronx. I undressed nervously, filled with performance anxiety, and quickly slid under the protective covers. Helene, in the meantime, was in the bathroom, getting ready. Getting ready for what? I was unsure. After quite some time, she came into the room, looking sexy in a lacy white negligee. She quickly slid under the covers, and before long, we two virgins were doin' what comes naturally. My nerves were relieved as I happily rose to the occasion, which turned out to be a rewarding experience for us both. But before my happy ending, she stopped everything, turned on the lights, and proceeded to show me her blood on the sheet. She had vowed to be a virgin bride, and she wanted me to know it.

Next morning, we were off for a week's honeymoon at the Nevele Hotel in the Catskill Mountains. It was a lovely hotel, mostly populated by fellow Jews, and in good Jewish mother tradition, the food was plentiful. And unlike my own mother's cooking, it was quite good. I was happy during our stay. We ice-skated, shopped in the quaint little town nearby, took lots of pictures, and met another honeymoon couple who were fun to be with. The groom was very good-looking, and I thought to myself that he too would *really* be fun to be with. Every afternoon, there would be an announcement over the loudspeaker, informing us honeymooners that it was time to return to our rooms and "wash our socks," code words for lovemaking. In most cases, we happily took him up on the offer.

Chapter 3

NO BIZ LIKE SHOW BIZ

Helene and I moved out of the Bronx and found a cute one-bedroom apartment in Kew Gardens, Queens. The area wasn't as old as Pelham Parkway, and it was a definite step up. My buddy, Paul Langer, and his wife, Fran, moved into the adjoining building shortly after our move. It was nice having them around. Great people, and we would double date every now and then.

After all those years in fear of my father, once I moved out of the house, he became a pussy cat. Since I was born nine years after my brother, it seemed obvious to me that I was a surprise. Another mouth to feed that got in the way of his gambling. He resented me, and it showed. But the new Murray Green was easy to take, and I just went along with it for what it was worth. But I never forgot.

Not long after the move, things became difficult. I bounced around from job to job, and I had only my insecurity to blame. I still had unresolved fears about people, and each new job brought up new people and new fears. I was afraid this one or that one didn't like me, and there was no justification for feeling that way, just the old tapes being replayed in my head. All kinds of weird thoughts prevented me from sticking to one job and making a go of it, and it was unnerving!

It was time to see a psychiatrist (my very first!) to get to the bottom of that irrational behavior and also, of course, to discuss my marriage and my sexuality. Helene didn't know about the sexuality part, and when I would come home, she was filled with questions. The actor in me came shining through, and Helene remained unaware of my homosexual leanings.

My shrink wasn't much of a help emotionally, but he helped me in a most unexpected way. The vastly unpopular Vietnam War was going on, and wouldn't you know, I got a "greetings" correspondence from nobody's favorite uncle—Uncle Sam! I was panicky. I turned to my shrink and asked him to write me a letter saying that because of a nervous condition, I was unfit for army duty. Thankfully, he obliged. I went to the recruiting office and gave the performance of my life. Twitching, shaking, stuttering, the works, and it worked! I walked out a free man!

After fleeing job after job, I felt like an absolute failure as a husband to Helene, a failure to her parents, and most of all, to myself. I found it hard to face her parents. In fact, it was hard to face just about everyone in my life. I was in a state of turmoil. I had to get away, but I had nowhere to turn. And so I signed myself in for thirty days at Creedmoor, a mental hospital. Being there, if only for thirty days, kept me free from worrying about the cruel, cold world outside. But unfortunately, it did nothing to permanently alter my frightened state of mind. Compared to the other patients, I was totally together! Most others were there for drug problems, and when tranquilizers were handed out, the patients would come to me begging for a little fix. I did make friends with a very young gay fellow whose name escapes me now. We would chat long into the night, and all I remember is his having had a very nasty childhood with parents who turned their backs on him. That's all I recall about Creedmoor. It served merely as a temporary Band-Aid, and that's about all I can say for it.

Home at last, and at a loss, I decided to pursue my original dream of becoming an actor. One thing I can say for Helene; she was compassionate and understanding. We never discussed Creedmoor again. However, when I discussed going to drama school, she was dead set against it. I stuck to my guns, and Helene and I separated while I attended the Herbert Berghof school of drama in Greenwich Village. While we were apart, I moved back into my parents' home. Where else would I go? Anyway, school turned out to be a shattering experience and a real dream breaker for me. There I was, in class with a group of young people who, for the most part, were totally into Shakespeare. I was more the Tennessee Williams type. Remember my early home life? Very Tennessee Williams! Anyway, I felt inferior to my high-minded classmates, and when I recited my monologue, which came from a modern crime caper, I was shaking to the core. I was convinced that I had made a fool out of myself, and I never went back.

During that period, Helene was staying with her parents, also in the Bronx. One night I visited her, and we took a walk together, winding up in a local high school football field, and there we made love. Shortly after, we were living together again.

My future plans were at a standstill until I read a news article about the field of court reporting. It piqued my interest, and before long, I was taking classes in night school. In order to build up my speed, I decided to seek a full-time job using the stenotype machine, and as luck would have it, I found that job as a secretary at 20th Century-Fox Film

Corporation. When I interviewed, it became clear that there were no male secretaries there, but I guess my enthusiasm and great interest in films saved the day, and I was hired on the spot. It must have been providence.

Helene was not pleased. She had a strong jealous streak, and the thought of my working in the film industry made her go bonkers. She was sure I would link up with some lovely starlet and head for the hills of Hollywood, or wherever the hills might take us. There I was, struggling with my sexual identity, and Helene was afraid I'd take off with some exotic chick. Life can be very strange at times, don't you think?

Helene became increasingly insecure. She had nothing to worry about, of course, and I loved my new job. I worked for an executive named Claude Lewis Jr., who was a terrific boss. He was a tall, handsome black man with a sharp, biting wit, and I strongly suspected that he was gay. He lived alone in Greenwich Village, he dressed immaculately, and his sense of humor kept us all happy. Oh yes, and he also made plenty of implications about my own sexuality. It became a game of cat and mouse, and I enjoyed it tremendously.

Charles Glenn was another rising executive who shared an office with Claude. He was a riot—a good-looking, recently married young fellow who loved to do imitations of famed celebrities, especially Margaret Hamilton, the Witch in *The Wizard of Oz*. He had her down to a *t*, and he put on quite an entertaining show.

Sitting beside me were two young gals, Linda Cifuni and another Linda whose last name escapes me. They were adorable, and we got along like gangbusters. Once or twice a week, we would go to lunch together with a couple of guys from other departments, Carl Molica from the photo division and Dennis Preato from the art department. Dennis became one of my oldest and dearest friends, a wonderful guy with a sly sense of humor and an astonishing knowledge of early movie history.

As it turned out, I performed over and above the call of duty. Claude might have a question about the movies or sometimes Charles would be in a bind over some ad copy, and I was only too willing to help. They appreciated and valued my input, and for the first time ever on any job, I felt like I truly belonged.

Approximately one year later, Johnny Friedkin was hired to head the advertising/publicity department, and he was in need of an executive secretary. Before I knew it, I was promoted and working for Johnny (we all called him Johnny). He was a nice guy with a truckload of movie experience, and I was thrilled to work for him. Before I knew it, people from the publicity department were asking me to help out with writing press releases. They seemed to be happy with my work, and they came to me with regularity. I was extremely self-satisfied, and I wanted to stay on the job forever. Helene was still uncomfortable with me in showbiz, but I was not going to leave when I'd found myself in a place where I felt happy and secure. Fox had some great product being released at the time, and I was proud to be a part of the scene and to hear inside stories about various productions.

One of our releases was *The Sweet Ride*, starring Anthony Franciosa, Michael Sarrazin, and Jacqueline Bisset. I wrote a syndicated feature about the film, and one of the top executives at the Associated Press sent my story back to Johnny with a note telling him how much he enjoyed my work. I could hardly believe it. Johnny made it a point to show me the rave review, and before I knew it, he helped me land a job at United Artists as assistant publicity director. But despite the fact that the job would pay twice what I was making at Fox, I pleaded with him to let me stay. I felt so comfortable, and I didn't want to upset my cart. I may have been praised and leaned upon for help in other areas of the business, but deep down inside, I still felt like the insecure kid who was destined to fail. But as they say, when you gotta go, you gotta go. So I went.

At United Artists (UA), I worked for Mike Gray, head of publicity. I even had my own secretary, but to be honest, I felt that he (yes, it was a guy) was more qualified than myself. Fred Skidmore was the kind of guy everybody took an instant shine to. He was blond, good-looking, and exuded confidence. He too was gay, but he didn't come out to me until years later. I don't think I performed very well on that job. The staff meetings were grueling for me as I felt self-conscious in a room filled with my peers, and I contributed little to the meetings. One of my fellow publicists was Jonathan Demme, who became a renowned film director. As I recall, he was very bright, enthusiastic, and an all-around nice guy. Everything I hoped to be.

I never cheated on Helene. But I guess you might call it my fantasy cheat when I would trot myself over to Times Square during some lunch hours (Times Square was really lurid back in the '60s!), go into one of the many porno shops that lined the streets, and pick up a copy of *Physique Pictorial,* or any of the other magazines that showed beautiful men posed in the skimpiest outfits the law would allow. Before I dared open one, I would look nervously from side to side to make sure nobody I knew was around, and that's how I would get my cheap thrills at the time. I wasn't proud, and I would feel guilty as hell afterward, but it became a compulsion, and it was the only way I could revel in that part of me I had kept hidden for so long.

One of the projects I worked on was a film entitled *The Night They Raided Minsky's*. One of the show girls in the film, Gloria LeRoy, a lady who had toured for many years with Ann Corio's burlesque show, invited me to the Corio show, which was having a run at the Westbury Music Fair on Long Island. Helene and I went, and it turned out to be a night to remember. There we were, sitting in the theatre, enjoying the show when, all of a sudden, out came Gloria. She had a mink wrapped around her lovely shoulders, and that was pretty much the extent of her wardrobe. She pointed to a few men in the orchestra and said, "Hello, Sammy! Hello, Doug! Hello, Howard!" Well, that did it! Helene turned red as a beet. At intermission, she stormed out of the theatre with me trailing close behind. She dashed to the nearest bus stop, cursed me out like a drunken sailor, and accused me of having an affair with the burlesque queen. I'd never heard such language coming out of her! She took the bus, and I took my seat and watched the remainder of the show. When I got home that evening, I reassured her that nothing was going on, and thankfully, it didn't take long to make things right. Makeup sex works wonders!

Helene and I had a nice, healthy sex life, but it almost came to an abrupt halt when we received an unforgettable phone call from our upstairs neighbor. She complimented Helene and me on the frequency of our lovemaking, and then she let me have it when she said, "Do you guys really have to make so much noise when you're making love?" I ended the conversation as quickly as I could, and told Helene. She was devastated. She began to sob uncontrollably, and it took quite some time before I convinced her that this woman meant nothing to us, and it would be foolish to move.

But I still had my job and my insecurities to contend with. I heard about an opening at Paramount Pictures and, needing to escape from the discomfort I felt at UA, I interviewed for a job with publicity head Howard Newman. Before long, I was working at Paramount as a trade press contact. That was another job I enjoyed. The trade press, in general, was a nice bunch of guys. I would meet and greet them at our advance screenings, I would send out press releases, and I was there for them in any way possible. While there, I worked with a fellow named Jack Lyons. He was obviously gay, and we became close friends. Another plus on the job was getting to work with some top-level celebrities. At the time, Jack Lemmon was probably my favorite male film actor. He was shooting a movie for us entitled *The Out-of-Towners,* a very funny comedy in which he costarred with Sandy Dennis. It was my job to accompany him, his manager, and Eric Silver, a writer for *Variety*, to lunch for an exclusive interview. That was quite a lunch. Not only was I impressed by the very nice Mr. Lemmon, but Eric, a good-looking fellow, was as interested in playing footsies with me under the table as he was in talking to Lemmon. I can't say enough about Jack Lemmon. He was as down-to-earth as can be and even insisted that I get driven back to work in his shared limo. When it was time for him and his wife to return to their home in California, he gave me the stereo player that Paramount had given him for his stay in New York. Quite a guy!

On another occasion, I was assigned to pick up Clint Eastwood, star of our upcoming film *Paint Your Wagon*, at Kennedy Airport. He arrived with a couple of friends. We hopped into the limo, and I found Eastwood to be not only incredibly good-looking but also incredibly nice. He was, in fact, one of the nicest celebrities I've ever had the pleasure of working with. The next day, Clint and I lunched at Sardi's, a famous theatrical restaurant in the heart of the theatre district. He ordered steak tartare, and I decided to do the same. I didn't realize that the dish was raw chopped meat, and so I reluctantly picked at it, hoping that Clint wouldn't notice how little I actually ate. Later, at the restaurant, he was interviewed by one of my trade press contacts. Eastwood was not the most talkative guy, but what he had to say was golden. Shortly thereafter, he was off to Yugoslavia to do a war film entitled *Kelly's Heroes.* Six or seven months later, at the premiere of *Paint Your Wagon,* he arrived with his wife, saw me at the after-party, immediately smiled, and said, "Hi, Howard!" I was very impressed. This guy is the real deal. It's no wonder the same production people worked for him year after year.

Through industry friends, I met an elegant older lady named Viola Rubber, who had coproduced the Broadway hit, *Night of the Iguana* in 1961, and had been in charge of casting for numerous productions during the '50s. We hit it off immediately, and once a month or so, we would meet for lunch at the Wellington Hotel in Manhattan. On one occasion, she invited me to attend singer Shirley Bassey's opening night at the Waldorf Astoria. We sat front and center at a table for Bassey's guests, and I had the pleasure of sitting between two actors I had admired, Jack Klugman and Estelle Parsons. They were delightful people, but Klugman was mooching cigarettes from me non-stop throughout the evening. He was diagnosed with throat cancer in 1974, however, his voice was not the same. It was raspy and quiet. I couldn't help but think of that night when he smoked my cigarettes incessantly. It saddened me to hear the news.

Chapter 4

HAVING A GAY OLD TIME

'll never forget the phone call I got from my aunt Julia. We were talking, and she was babbling on about something that meant little to me. Well, she just went on and on, and finally, in exasperation, I hung up on her. Just a few weeks later, she had a fatal heart attack. I remember the call to this day, and I regret not having made peace with her.

Things were going along well at Paramount. Jack Lyons and I became good friends, and I continued to enjoy my role as trade press contact. One evening, our boss had Jack and me over to his apartment for dinner where he regaled us with many stories about the films and the stars he had worked with. For all I know, he may have had me over because he suspected that I was one of the "gang," the gay gang. Whatever the case, it was a fun evening, and months later, Howard Newman passed away. What a loss!

After a while, we moved out of the Paramount building on Seventh Avenue to the brand-new Gulf and Western Building on West Fifty-Ninth Street (it now stands as Trump International Hotel and Tower-New York). Jack and I shared an office in our new digs, and we had a great view of the city. It was fun in that new setting, but the fun was short-lived. Things were taking a 360 degree turn at home. Helene's psychiatrist had only met me once, and it was a brief hello, good-bye, but after hearing from Helene about my early home life, she implied that I might have "sexual identity problems." Wow! Talk about good perception! I'll never forget the evening it all came to the fore. As usual, Helene and I were having milk and cake a few hours after dinner. In a most matter-of-fact manner, she asked me, "Howard, do you have sexual identity problems?" I was flabbergasted. I didn't know quite what to do or say, so I fell off my chair, landed on the floor, and began to laugh. That happens sometimes. I didn't know whether to laugh or cry, so I chose the former. In about three seconds flat, I got back up on my chair and decided that it was now or never. Time to let it all hang out. I'd never been untruthful (or unfaithful) to Helene, my little secret aside; and since that was nearly out, it was time to swing that closet door wide open!

I really loved Helene, and we discussed the situation in a civilized manner. She wanted me to get help. Help-shmelp. I wanted to get some same-sex action. I didn't want a divorce. I told Helene that since it was out in the open, I would have to see what it was all about. I wanted to stay with her and hopefully work things out, but when I told her that I needed to test the water, she cried out, "Oh, no. You're not going to get me sick!" Well, that, unfortunately, was that. It was time to move on, time, after twenty-eight years, to go and find myself.

The next evening, I packed my bags and took off for the Big City. Not having much dough, I rented a room at the Westside YMCA. I didn't realize it was a gay mecca, but anything short of blindness could tell you that in an instant. There I was, a freshly minted, officially out-of-the-closet gay guy, and there they were, men all over the place with a look in their eyes that spelled S-E-X. I was scared to death. I checked in quickly, very quickly, and next thing I knew I was in a sad little room on the phone with Eric Silver, my little footsie friend from *Variety* who had been lusting after me for years. I told him about the split, and he asked me to come right over. I was nervous as I entered his small apartment in Greenwich Village, but it didn't take long for me to calm down and get down to business. Funny, after hiding my sexuality all those years, it all came very naturally to me. I wasn't at all ill at ease, and the evening was memorable.

I couldn't spend another night at the Y, so my next move was back to the Bronx with Mom and Pop. They just couldn't understand why Helene and I had split, and I sure as hell wasn't ready to tell them.

Meanwhile, back at Paramount Pictures, just when I was settling in to my new quarters, I was called in to Marilyn Steven's office. She was the new publicity director, taking the place of Howard Newman. No one in the department cared much for her. She had plenty of attitude, and on top of it, we all thought she was a phony. She motioned for me to have a seat, and then proceeded to fire me. "Oh, great," I mumbled to her. "First I'm separated from my wife, and now I'm fired. Wonderful." Guess I was trying to make her feel guilty. I forgot; you need a heart to feel that way. Stewart said, "I'm sorry," but sorry just didn't cut it. Everything was crashing around me.

But on the plus side, I was basking in my new life, and I felt surprisingly liberated. It was a wonderful feeling to be able to talk about myself without guilt. For the first time in my life, I was happy to be *me*. Jack Lyons was a godsend. He took me around to the latest happening gay bars in town and introduced me to a bunch of nice guys. My first time in a gay bar was not at all what I expected. I didn't realize how many flavors of gay there were in the world. Everything from good-looking Rock Hudson types to boys next door to businessmen in suits to limp-wristed Liberaces! I felt a bit intimidated, but that didn't last long due to the friendliness of the crowd, and my friend Jack beside me all the way didn't hurt either. Having been in a conventional marriage with Helene, I thought my story would be fascinating to the guys, but I couldn't have been more disillusioned. So many gays have been married, many of them with children. That evening proved to be a real eye-opener!

Since then I had to get myself a divorce lawyer. For a while, Helene didn't really get what was happening. I flew to California to attend the wedding of my cousin Karen, and Helene asked if I was taking her. "We're separated, Helene. No, I'll be going on my own," I replied. A bit curt, now that I think of it, but I had to make the point; and before long, Helene had a lawyer of her own. We could have settled things in a well-balanced, fair way. I was willing to help her as best I could, but having lawyers getting involved is not pretty. I thought Helene and I were on good terms, but when we got together with our respective lawyers, it was *war!* Don't know where she got him, but her lawyer was a rabid pit bull. He managed to milk me for approximately $350 per month alimony, and there I was without a job. Helene claimed that she was in no condition to be working, and as I recall, I think she got her shrink to attest to that. I was not a happy camper.

Living at Mom's and going out most nights to the city was not the easiest way out, but for the time being, it was necessary. Eventually, I bagged a job in publicity back at my old stomping grounds, 20th Century-Fox. Only at that time, I worked in the television department. I fit in very well there and made good friends with my coworkers, David Young and Larry Lederman, two stand-up guys who were also members of the club.

My boss, Joe Fusco Jr., had a great sense of humor, and eventually, he too became a friend. All it took was one weekend in Chicago. He and I went there on business, and we stayed at the Pick Congress Hotel. We only had one free evening to spend there, and we had dinner together—great steaks—directly across from the Stock Yards. Then we wound up in Joe's suite where we smoked a little weed. Well, I loosened up like a wet rag, and evidently, I was very funny. I kept Joe in stitches, and we were fast friends from then on. I'll never forget the wonderful ice cream Joe introduced me to at the hotel. It was so good that we both had it shipped in dry ice to our homes. What a treat!

Back in New York, I continued to make the rounds, usually with Jack Lyons. He was very outgoing, and being with him made it easy to meet new people. But after just a few months, I was getting tired of the scene. I'm really not the type to jump from one bed to another, and ideally, I was hoping to meet someone I could share my life with. Enter Joe Southard. I was at a dance bar when I spied Joe. He had all the attributes I liked in a guy. He had a good sense of humor; he was well-toned, and he had a great little butt! He asked me to dance (that was during the disco craze), and we chatted long afterward. He was intelligent and charming, and before long, we were off to his apartment on East Eighty-Fourth Street. His place was very impressive. Not only was it beautifully decorated, but the view of the skyline from his terrace was magnificent. Last, but not least, we really hit a home run in the sack. I was sold.

I was hoping to see more of Joe, and as luck would have it, he seemed to be as interested in me as I was in him. We saw each other regularly for a couple of months, and it was a nice time in my life. The job was going well, and things were looking up until Joe invited me to a party at his friend Bud Greenberg's house. The place was jumping. Wall-to-wall guys, plenty to drink, and smoke (this *was* the seventies); and for a while, I was having a great time. Then

I happened to look across the room, and there was Joe, seriously smooching with some other guy! At that, I walked up to my host, thanked him (very quickly) for a wonderful evening, and turned on my heels without saying a word to Joe. I took the subway home feeling very dejected and vowing to never see Joe again.

After a couple of glum weeks, he called me at my mom's place. I told him I couldn't really talk there, and I went out to call him from a neighborhood phone booth. I really let him have it. I told him how insensitive I felt his actions were, and that I didn't want to see him again. Well, Joe had great persuasive power, and it didn't take very long before I found myself back in his arms. In fact, we started seeing one another with even more regularity, and not long afterward, I was living the good life on the chichi East Side of New York City.

Joe had a wonderful circle of friends—Bud Greenberg, Bob Stigwood, Tommy Dineen, Jack Jason, and a few gay gals as well. We were very social. On top of his other attributes, Joe was a gourmet cook, and we entertained regally. I learned so much during that period. My days and nights were filled with good friends at work, good friends after hours, dining in fine restaurants, and entertaining at home with elaborate dinner parties. On top of it, Joe even taught me how to eat European style. It's really much simpler than our American method, and you don't have to switch hands between cutting and eating. I was in eighth heaven, one step above seventh.

One of the gals we hung out with was a gorgeous, feminine gay gal named Veronica. Ladies who fit this description are often referred to as "lipstick lesbians." Like me, she was born in the Bronx, and we hit it off just as soon as we met. On a number of occasions, I needed a date to accompany me at work functions, and Virginia was my obvious choice. At these affairs, my jealous coworkers would come up to me and ask where I found such a beauty. I told them it was a secret, and she and I had some good laughs over this on the way home.

Chapter 5

CALIFORNIA, HERE I COME!

A few months after we met, Joe lost his very good job at a computer firm, and after a few months of unemployment, he bagged himself a position as a bartender at one of New York's most popular gay bars. I was not thrilled. But you gotta do what you gotta do, and I took it in stride. Joe worked until closing time, which was approximately 3:00 a.m., and I spent many evenings alone. But we still managed to enjoy a good social life, and even though he was surrounded by some of the hottest gay guys in New York City, I never mistrusted him until one evening. Instead of his coming home at his usual 4:00 a.m., he arrived at 5:30 a.m. I didn't start a fight, but I recall when he walked into the bedroom, I sat up, arms folded, and said, "Have a nice time, Joe?" That's as far as it went. I don't know to this day if anything occurred, but we sailed smoothly ahead with our lives. Having been brought up in a home where fighting was the order of the day, I did anything to avoid a fight. I'm that way to this day.

Things were going great at my job, but a big change was coming. It was announced that we were going to be relocated to the 20th Century-Fox Studio in Beverly Hills, California. The thought intrigued me. I had family there— my dear cousin Karen, my aunt Joan, and my uncle Irving. Plus, I thought a change would be fun, and it would get Joe out of that damned bar! Joe went right along with the program, as he had lived in LA at one time, and he had lots of friends there. He seemed as eager as I was.

Then it was time to break the news to my mom. I'll never forget it. After I told her, she shook her head from side to side and said, "Do you mean to tell me they're sending you to California and they know you have a mother here in New York? What kind of people are they?" That's my mom! California, here I come!

In December of 1973, we arrived in San Francisco. There we picked up a white 1972 Cadillac DeVille convertible, which a friend sold to us at a greatly reduced price. And so we traversed scenic Route 1 to Los Angeles in high style. Driving through beautiful Monterey County was a great way to begin our California adventure, and the palm trees lined up against a full moon and reflected in the still waters of the Pacific Ocean took my breath away. I was very impressed. The surrounding mountainside was beautiful, and it was December. The temperature during the day was in the high eighties. What's not to like?

Before we found our own place, Joe and I stayed at Will Wright's guest house in Nichols Canyon. Will was a fabulous guy. I'd say he was in his late fifties or early sixties, and he had a great sense of humor. And although he was famous for his upscale chain of ice cream parlors, he was as down-to-earth as anyone. He lived with his lover, a handsome young Latino named John Muniz, and both of them were perfect hosts. It was a good beginning. The guest house was warm and cozy, and I was ready to embark on my career in Hollywood! I even experienced my first earthquake at that house. Just days after we arrived, the ground began to shake. I ran to the window to see what was happening outside, but it all looked pretty safe to me. I wasn't scared; I was fascinated. Everything at the time just seemed new and exciting!

First day on the Fox lot, I drove through to be greeted with a friendly "good morning" by none other than actor Steve McQueen. Later that same day, I saw Paul Newman strolling by, and a week later, Richard Chamberlain and I had a friendly good-morning chat. It seemed to me that

I was really going to like it here. Newman and McQueen were shooting a multimillion-dollar flick (in those days, that figure was astonishing!) called *The Towering Inferno*. I had my own parking space, a nice-size cubicle, and I shared the room with David and Larry, who had their own respective cubicles. So far, so good. Joe Fusco decided not to come out to LA, so for the first couple of weeks, we had no leader. But it didn't take long before we were introduced to the new publicity director, Fifi Booth. She appeared to be friendly enough and capable, but first impressions don't always count! In fact, they can be quite deceiving, particularly in this case. I'm all for women having equal rights and equal pay in the workplace, but there are some women who just don't handle their lofty positions well. Ms. Booth was a case in point. She seemed to feel that she had to be more masculine in order to prove herself capable, and at times, it got pretty annoying.

The first few months went along smoothly enough. I was still dazzled by my new surroundings, Joe and I were happy to be where we were, and all seemed swell in La-La Land. Joe introduced me to his friends, and they were a colorful bunch. In fact, his best friend there in LA was a fellow named Bob Myers. Remember Auntie Mame? Well, my new flamboyant friend Bob was her male counterpart. He was a highly successful interior decorator, and he had a fabulous home in West Hollywood. He was kind enough to throw us a "welcome to LA" party, and like everything else up to that point, it was razzly and dazzly. He had a tent set up in his backyard and roving waiters with hors d'oeuvres on sterling-silver trays. The drinks were flowing, and I was delighted to meet Joe's friends. One in particular, mega-producer Ross Hunter and his partner of many years, Jacques Mapes, were two of the guests, and I'll never forget Joe's way of introducing us. "Oh, Ross, this is Howard. And if you're not careful, he'll back you off into a corner and talk your ears off about Doris Day." And that's exactly what I did. Ross Hunter had produced some of Ms. Day's most successful films, *Pillow Talk, Midnight Lace,* and *Lover Come Back.* He was charming, unassuming, and more than happy to discuss Doris with me. He obviously adored her, and when I asked him when she'd return to the big screen, he replied that she seems to be content to just be resting on her laurels. I hoped that he was wrong, but as it turned out, he was so right. Ms. Day left the business, never looked back, and became a highly influential animal advocate.

That party was just the first of many elegant gatherings to come. Joe's friends were very upscale, and they were lots of fun. There was Charles Beacher, also a prominent decorator, and his lover, Gary Gray, who was a hairdresser and a sweetheart of a guy. Add Howard Hollis to the mix, a tall blond fellow who was extremely nice, and his lover, Billy. Billy owned a high-toned beauty shop in Beverly Hills, and we enjoyed some sumptuous dinners at their home. Some ladies were also in the group, Beverly and Jackie and Mokihana (she had played Bloody Mary in many touring productions of *South Pacific*) became good friends. The partygoers were a lively bunch (fueled by tons of liquor), and a good time seemed to be had by all, including me. With all the drinking we did at those shindigs and then driving home, it's a wonder we all came out of it alive.

In a short time, Joe landed a big job with a computer firm, and for a while, he was happy and living the good life right along with me. Dinner parties, cocktail parties, dining at fine restaurants, meeting sophisticated people, and having a job that I loved was intoxicating.

One day at work, I grabbed Larry and said, "We're going to Nate'n Al's delicatessen for lunch today." It was a popular haunt in Beverly Hills, and thanks to a number of fan magazine articles, I knew that Doris Day would often go there for brunch. We arrived at the deli, and the first thing I noticed was a bike parked outside. I began to get nervous. Doris always rode her bike through Beverly Hills, and I jittered my way through the door with Larry close behind. Son of a gun! There she was in all her glory and looking wonderful. My heart leapt with joy. While we waited for our table, I stared at Doris through a shelf full of canned goods. What a sight I must have been! Finally, we were seated, and I just couldn't be in the same restaurant as Doris without going over to say something, anything, to her. So I shook my way across the room and approached the woman I had idolized for practically my entire life. I was honest and open with her. "I just couldn't be in the same restaurant with you without saying something, so I'd like to wish you a happy belated birthday." It was about a week after her fifty-first, and she looked up at me and said, "How did you know it was my birthday?" to which I replied, "You'd be surprised at how much I know about you." "Oh!" she said. I then told her how happy I was to see her, and I walked, with my heart beating rapidly, all the way back to my table. Larry and I enjoyed our lunch, and after fifteen minutes or so, Doris waved at me from across the room. Now *that* was a day I won't soon forget.

Meanwhile, back at Nichols Canyon, it was time for Joe and me to find a place of our own. In a short time, we found a charming apartment just north of Sunset Boulevard in the heart of West Hollywood, sometimes referred to as boys' town. Actress-singer Lisa Kirk lived below us with her hubby, song writer Robert Wells, who cowrote "The Christmas Song" ("Chestnuts roasting on an open fire…") with Mel Tormé. And next door to us were the Moisos, a colorful couple who seemed to be counting the minutes each day until cocktail hour. They were eccentric but never dull. They'd pop in often, and we always had fun sipping our cool drinks and telling tall tales. I'll never forget when they had joint facelifts. For a week or so, they were bandaged up like a pair of mummies, and I must say they came out of their wrappings looking good.

Once settled in, we often had dinner parties at our place. One evening, we entertained Ross Hunter and Jacques. I was very excited at having them over, and I put the soundtrack of their film *Thoroughly Modern Millie* on the stereo just to make them feel warm and welcome as they arrived. They reciprocated the invitation, and we enjoyed a wonderful dinner at their place. I looked, of course, for some sign of Doris Day around the house, and I was happy to see a large photo of her in a scene from their very successful production of *Midnight Lace*. There were eight of us for dinner, including actress Margaret Lindsay and her girlfriend, and after dinner we watched a film. As I recall, it was a Western, not one of my favorite genres, but in that setting, I enjoyed it just the same.

Talk about wanting to redo something in life, Hunter invited me to join his bridge club, and I, like a jerk, said I don't play and that I'm not really a big card-playing fan. Little did I know that that was one of the most sought-after invitations in Hollywood. Rock Hudson played, Claire Trevor played, and I was told that anybody who was anybody wanted to be a part of that group. A missed opportunity for sure.

During that period, I heard about a class called Mind Expansion. A friend had attended and he praised it to the skies. Still riddled with self-doubts, I thought this might be a good way to gain some self-confidence. The class involved meditation, going from beta to alpha to the theta (deepest) state of mind. Once there, it was time to feed positive images and statements into the mind. The theory was that doing that continually, day after day, month after month was the path to mental health. I practiced diligently, and in time learned one of my greatest life lessons: being sad, depressed, and feeling insecure is like any bad habit. And bad habits can be replaced over time by good ones. Those positive meditations were a big help. I can't say that I'm 100 percent there, but I gained so much from the classes, and I've learned to feed positive thoughts into my head to override the negative. When negative thinking comes into play, I turn it around as quickly as I can. It can be done, and I can attest to it. That has helped immeasurably in making my life a lot happier.

While in California, like a good Jewish boy, I would call Mama at least once a week, and I'd go back to New York once a year. I made a revealing discovery during one such visit. I hugged my mom, looked her straight in the eyes, and said, "I love you." Her reply? "Likewise." Likewise? At that moment, it occurred to me. My mother couldn't say the words "I love you," and it saddened me to realize that she never said it to me at all. The same applies to my father. Never heard the words. To this day, when I see a dad holding his child and being tender and affectionate, it brings a lump to my throat. Despite that, I never doubted my mother's love.

Me and cousin Paul Kranz circa 1946

(top row from left) mom and Aunt Julia
(bottom row) brother Phil and me.

Me at age 12.

(Top row from left) Marvin Kaufman and Michael Katzoff
(Center row from left) Allen Stutz, Bruce Rund,
Marty Markowitz and Me
(Bottom Row) Mel Citrin and Ira Rosenberg

Me and Helene circa 1964

(from left) Larry Lederman, David Young and me at
20th Century-Fox, New York, circa 1971

Me and Joe circa 1972.

Dad, Uncle Irving, Aunt Joan, Mom
Bottom row Me and my niece, Elisa.

(From left) My brother, Phil, my mother, Fay, My dad,
Murray, my niece Elisa and my sister-in-law Helen.

Me and Jerry circa 1982

Jerry, B&B owner & me in Canada for World's Fair, circa 1986.

Doris Day and me circa 1987

Me with cousins David and Karen Marcus.

Cousins Betty and Sid Cooper

(from left) Ralph Zeek and Jack Hewson.

Chapter 6

STARS IN MY EYES

The walls were beginning to close in on me. First, I lost my job at Fox. Fifi Booth was no fan of mine. She knew that I (and the others) was not too crazy about her. She needed all the help she could get, so one by one, like ten little Indians, we were let go one at a time. I had the distinction of being the first. On top of that, things were not going well on the home front. Joe also lost his job, and our sex life wasn't much to talk about either. His needs in the sex department were not as strong as mine, and I was beginning to feel a bit frustrated.

During that bleak period, Joe and I were invited to spend a ski weekend on Bear Mountain with friends. That coincided with an American Film Institute television tribute to James Cagney, and I knew that Doris Day was going to be one of the guests. I wanted to tape-record the show (this was before DVR), so I bowed out of the weekend, and told Joe to go ahead and have a good time. Big mistake. I think Joe had a better time than I had anticipated. There was a successful choreographer named Carl Jablons, who had recently joined our group of friends. I'm not sure of it, but I strongly suspect that he and Joe did more than ski over that weekend. But then again, I was no angel myself. That very same weekend, my friend Howard Hollis invited me to his place for dinner. As it turned out, his lover had also gone on the ski trip, and the two of us had a little fling. I was extremely nervous. For three and a half years, I had been faithful to Joe (sort of), and when I was about to commit an unfaithful act, my nerves got the better of me, and my knees were doing the jitterbug. Once I calmed down, we made a score. It was nothing more than a one-timer, and it was really out of character for me. But things at home were not as they once were, and the writing had been on the proverbial wall for some time.

There was one other time when I was unfaithful. I visited New York every year to see Mom, and of course, I saw old friends as well. After a nice dinner and visit with my pal Jack Jason, I left his place, feeling no pain. We had had many drinks that evening, and we smoked a little grass. So there I was, three sheets to the wind, walking to the subway station. On the way, I passed a good-looking guy. He passed me. I looked back. He looked back. Before I knew it, we were on his couch, screwing the night away. He asked to see me again, but I didn't want that brief fling to be any more than that. Joe was still my guy, but not for long. That experience taught me a good lesson. I was the kind of guy least likely to cheat on a lover, but I did. And if I did it, I think almost any guy, under the right circumstances, would do the same. It must be in our DNA. Not long after, Joe gave me the "let's be friends" speech. I may have seen it coming, but it's never easy, and Joe and I spent a great part of that evening in tears. We held onto each other, but it didn't make things any easier, not for me and probably not for Joe. Neil Sedaka had it right: breaking up *is* hard to do!

So there I was, newly single, out of work, and looking for a place to stay. It didn't take long to find a great one-bedroom apartment on Hancock Avenue in West Hollywood, aka "the land of fruits and nuts." It was a very gay neighborhood and perfect for me since I was single. The rent was reasonable, and I had a fabulous view of the city! As soon as I saw that stunning view, I was sold.

Being on my own was a new experience for me, but I thoroughly enjoyed it. It was a great time to be out and about. I loved to dance, and the disco era was at its peak. There were great clubs throughout West Hollywood.

Nobody worried about catching a deadly disease, and the revelers paraded around the town as if tomorrow would never come. Since I was single and noticing how well-built the competition was, it was time for a makeover! First thing I did was enroll at the gym just around the corner from home. Can't make many lame excuses when the gym is practically at your doorstep. In addition to workouts at the gym, I took up power walking, and I've been participating in both activities ever since. At the gym, I struck up an acquaintance with a nice-looking blond fellow named Jack. He had obviously been working out for a long time as he was very well built, but not really my type. During one conversation, I asked what he did for a living. He told me that he was a dancer. He then added that he danced in the nude. Even though I'd been out for five years and I'd mixed with all types of guys, I couldn't hide my shocked expression at that revelation. "What?" I cried out. "How could you do that? Doesn't it make you nervous?" Little did I know that Jack went under the professional name of Jack Wrangler, and he was one of the most popular gay porn stars of the day. He told me that he mustered up the courage to dance by boozing it up before each performance. Months later, while walking down my street, I bumped into him. We stopped and chatted for a while, and then he asked if he could come up and "see my etchings."

I wasn't interested in canoodling with everyone's flavor of the month, so I quickly changed the subject and went on my way. In later years, he married one-time popular singer Margaret Whiting.

At my new digs, I made some good friends. There was Greg Wilson, who, to this day, is truly one of the sweetest guys I've ever met. He was very handsome but overweight. At one time, he had been a teen heartthrob with pictures in teen magazines and small parts in a number of movies in the '50s. He lived with his one-time partner, Ed Hummel, and though they were no longer lovers, their friendship was a close one. They had a long history together. Robie Sanders was another of my new-found friends, and he cut quite a dashing figure. He was tall, blond, charming, and made lasting impressions on just about everyone. I first laid eyes on Robie as I was leaving my building. He pulled up in his Caddy convertible and began to flirt. He then proceeded to invite me to dinner and to join him for comedienne Joan Rivers's show on the closing night of Ye Little Club, a long-time favorite spot in Beverly Hills. We had fun up to a point. Rivers was very funny, and by evening's end, I found myself in his apartment and, not much later, in his arms. Well, all charms aside, he had very bad breath. All it took was one kiss, and I was practically out the door. "I've got a really bad stomachache," I said and made a hasty exit.

He called the next day to inquire about my health, and I told him I was feeling better. But I let it be known that we could be good friends, and in time, we were.

Back in the '70s, bathhouses were a big draw for gay guys seeking out anonymous sex. A typical bath house would consist of a room displaying porno flicks just to get you in the mood or simply for lookie-loos and an orgy room, which would be pitch black and filled with thrill seekers who weren't interested in seeing any of their partners. Some guys would have a number of them each night. It was debauchery at its highest level. In some rooms, you might find a gay guy lying on his chest with his butt in the air like a sexy landing strip. Those guys weren't very discriminating, and just about anyone could enter the room and jump the guy's bones. Most rooms, however, were taken up by couples who simply wanted what some gays call "vanilla" sex, just plain ole huggin' and kissin' and doin' that ever-popular dance, the horizontal mambo. I wasn't really into the scene, but after one night of one drink too many, a friend coaxed me into going. Being a bit high, and after sniffing some amyl nitrate, I made my rounds with the de rigueur towel wrapped firmly around my waist. In my inebriated state, I saw a guy who really turned me on. I walked slowly up to him and had to laugh after I bumped my nose into what turned out to be my own image in a mirrored wall. That's how stoned I was. Shortly thereafter, I strolled into the orgy room, and before I knew it, I was holding a stranger whose finely chiseled body felt like that of a Greek god. Before I knew it, we were screwing, and after a bit of it and when my eyes adjusted to the dark, I could faintly see a number of peering eyes, looking down at our veiled by the dark images. Whaddya know? I'm in showbiz at last! Like I said, it really wasn't my thing, and it was the first and last time I entered such an establishment.

One memory I'll hold in my heart forever was the time I spent watching Doris Day as she taped her TV special, *Doris Day Today*. I read in the trade papers that an acquaintance of mine, Tony Charmoli, was assigned to direct Doris in a musical special for CBS-TV. That's all I had to know. In less than a New York minute, I was on the phone with Tony, and he graciously permitted me to visit the set at NBC Studios in Burbank. Before I went, I picked up a cute poodle-shaped Styrofoam figure dotted with licorice Nips candies. Playing on DD's love of animals and sweets, I thought that would be the perfect gift. I entered the sound stage, and there she was, looking absolutely stunning. She was fifty-three years old at the time with a body that a twenty-five-year-old would envy. I went right over to her and made my presentation. She smiled that great smile at me and gave me a kiss on the cheek. Later that day,

I joined her at the coffee percolator, and we chatted as we drank our coffee. I asked if she'd be singing any contemporary songs, and she said that she'd be singing "Day by Day," from the hit Broadway show *Godspell.* I was glad to hear it, and then I mentioned how much I loved her recording of the old Sammy Cahn classic also entitled "Day by Day." She began to sing it. Without thinking, I joined in, and before I knew it, we were halfway through a duet. Imagine that! Me duetting with Doris Day! Incredible. A short time later, she was called to the set to perform a novelty tune with John Denver. I watched a great deal of the taping, and the highlight for me was when I stood right beside the camera as Doris was singing "The Way We Were." Now Doris is notoriously afraid of singing in front of live audiences. Ever since the mid-'50s, she dropped live musical appearances completely and concentrated on her film career and recording in the safe confines of the Columbia Records studios. So my being there with Doris singing right in front of me was a rare treat that few fans get to experience. It remains a lifetime highlight for me.

It's funny. I'd been scared of cats all my life until the evening my pal Greg came knocking at my door. I opened it to find him with a stray cat in his arms, pleading with me to take in the little guy. I shouted, "No way!" and slammed the door in his face. Well, Greg wasn't about to give up so easily, and he continued to knock and ring my bell for a good ten minutes. Finally, I relented and let him in, but I kept my distance from the awful cat. Greg told me how the cat had followed him while he was walking his dog, and the animal was obviously friendly and in need of a friend himself. After much heated debate, I decided to keep the cat, "just for the night." Well, Charly turned out to be so sweet that we became fast pals. And "just for the night" turned out to be eighteen years. I soon discovered just why I had been so afraid of the feline population. I called my mom in New York to tell her the good news, and she said, "Ooooh, what do you want a cat for? Do you know a cat almost smothered your grandmother in her sleep?" Then I called my aunt Joan, and she repeated the same story. So that's what it was! That tale had been drummed into my dear little ear so often that I feared those furry little critters all my life. Charly turned out to be a great companion, and now I'm as big a cat lover as they come.

After a great deal of searching, I landed a publicity job at one of LA's most successful PR agencies, Solters & Roskin. This could have—should have—been the job of a lifetime, but even though I was well suited to it, my insecurity got the best of me and prevented me from making a life's career out of that great opportunity. The firm had an amazing list of clients: John Denver, Lucille Ball, and Barbra Streisand, just to name a few, and it was a thrilling step up for me. My first assignment was to cover a press interview between John Denver and a reporter for the *LA Times*. Denver was house-guesting at his agent Jerome Weintraub's fabulous home in Malibu, and that's where the interview took place. I was a little skeptical about John Denver before I met him. He just seemed a bit too good to be true with his songs of love, simplicity, and the great outdoors. But it didn't take long for me to see that this was a good man with a great deal of integrity. The interview went smoothly. Denver was never at a loss for words, and my job was to take note of anything I could use later as an exclusive feature or for a simple column item to feed the press.

Next, I was assigned to the queen of comedy, Lucille Ball. She was scheduled to do an interview in conjunction with a CBS-TV special commemorating her twenty-fifth anniversary on television. I arrived early at Lucy's home in Beverly Hills. She greeted me at the door and made me feel like an old friend. She was wonderful. I was accustomed to seeing her on TV, wearing extravagant red wigs and tons of makeup. But here, at home, she was just herself, and I must say, without the artificial accoutrements, she was more attractive than she had appeared on recent TV shows. I couldn't help but notice two important things.

Her doormat had a big letter M in the center. She was married to a comic named Gary Morton, and it was obvious that at home, Lucy wisely let Gary be the star. Over the fireplace was a large painting of Morton swinging a golf club. Lucy obviously went out of her way to make her husband feel equal to her. Good thinking. Theirs was a long, successful union. As we waited for the newspaper columnist, Lucy was chatty, and she regaled me with tales about her mom and how hard it is to find a good rest home for seniors. She hated the idea of CBS celebrating her twenty-five-year reign with the network. "Feels like a eulogy at my funeral," she said. She also talked about her TV sidekick, Vivian Vance, whom she missed terribly, and finally, after about half an hour, she asked me if I'd like to join her in a game of backgammon. I told her that I never played, and I'll never forget this. She looked me straight in the eye and said, "You look like you were *born* to play backgammon." What that meant, I'll never know, but it was fun being with her, and it's a page pressed firmly in my book of memories.

Since we represented Barbra Streisand, we worked in her backyard the night she held a fundraiser for her buddy, politician Bella Abzug. Lee introduced me to Streisand; we shook hands, and that was about the extent of it. However, later in the evening, I caught her staring at me. At that time in my life, I was constantly being compared looks-wise to actor

Omar Sharif. Streisand had appeared with him, and they allegedly had a brief affair while working on the film *Funny Girl*. I assumed that the stare was because of my similar look.

The job at Solters should have been a real game changer for me. I was good at my work, but I had a serious problem. Those old insecurities came shining through whenever I had to sit through a staff meeting. I was fine in all respects except when it came down to expressing myself in front of my peers. That old feeling of being judged by others was hard to shake. That, unfortunately, got in the way of my ever advancing as I should have in the film/TV industry. To put it plainly, I was afraid. Old habits really do die hard. It got so bad that I went up to Lee Solters and asked him to let me go. He didn't understand and said that he liked my work. I practically pleaded. I asked him to please make it appear as though I were let go and not fired so that I could receive my unemployment benefits. He was kind enough to do that for me, and that was that.

As always, I made my annual pilgrimage to New York to see family, friends, and the theatre in that order. While there, I remember being in a car with my brother Phil and telling him about my sexuality. I expected a big dramatic scene, but all I got from him was a nod, and he simply said, "Yeah, I know." To be honest, I was a bit disappointed. I expected it to be a big deal, but now, in hindsight, I'm happy it turned out that way. I never brought the subject up with my mom and dad. They were just too old school to really get it, or so I thought. However, during Anita Bryant's antigay period, my dad asked me, with a mischievous twinkle in his eye, what I thought of Anita Bryant. That's as close as he ever came to letting me know that he knew me better than I thought he did.

Chapter 7

NEW BEGINNINGS

The first time Joe came to my new place was days after my thirty-third birthday, and he surprised me with a beautiful Japanese *byobu* screen that I loved and have hanging in my living room to this day. In the course of conversation, he told me there was somebody new in his life. He added that it was funny because the new guy was more domineering than he was, to which I replied, "Who is it, Hitler?" We both cracked up, and I was proud of myself for that clever response. The new man in his life turned out to be choreographer Carl Jablons, as I had suspected. As Joe left, we chatted briefly at the door and then kissed, knowing that it would be our last. It was a long, hard kiss, and it was memorable, as it was intended to be.

Then out of work for a number of months, I decided to do some freelance writing. I know the *National Enquirer* did not have the best reputation, but I only became involved in writing good human nature stories. Nothing lurid or controversial for me. Many dispute the authenticity of their features, but when I worked for them, it was a ruling, strictly adhered to, that all interviews were to be tape-recorded, thus preventing lawsuits of any kind.

I had read a small column item about Johnny Mathis having donated an organ to his hometown church, and I thought it might make a good human interest story. A meeting was arranged, and I was introduced to Mathis at RoJon, his production office in Hollywood. Mathis was down-to-earth and as modest as can be. He mentioned that he learned a great deal about singing from his dad, who, he said, had a wonderful singing voice himself. When Clem Mathis heard his son singing, he bought an old upright piano for $25 and encouraged him. Johnny started singing and dancing for visitors at home, at school, and in church. As a show of appreciation to the church, he made the generous donation. That interview was a lovely two hours spent with a lovely, handsome man.

I also interviewed English character actress Hermione Baddeley. Since she had appeared in two films with Doris Day, I couldn't help but ask how she liked working with her.

She liked Doris all right, but she thought very little of her husband, Martin Melcher. He coproduced the two films in which she worked, *Midnight Lace* and *Do Not Disturb*. She was not happy with the camera angles he insisted upon to highlight Doris and which left Hermione with her back to the camera. It's no surprise that industry insiders referred to him as Farty Belcher. The crux of the article was her desire to never play leading lady roles, but nice, juicy characters instead. Being a character actress was her forte, and the quirkier the character, the better she liked it. She was a delightful old gal.

Since I had some time on my hands, I became very close to my neighbors, Greg and Robie. They were fun to be with. We'd get together by the pool, and we would often go out to dinner. Greg, a down-to-earth guy, and Robie, who liked to think of himself as a bon vivant, clashed often, but the friendship remained. Robie would always remark about Greg's unorthodox style of eating. He'd put butter in his gourmet soup and he ate as though he were having a race, but that didn't matter to me. He was the kindest guy I'd ever met, and since he's been gone, I hold his memory dearly in my heart.

Greg lived with his long-time friend, Ed Hummel, and the two opened a health food store called Aunt Tillie's in the Pacific Design Center in West Hollywood. The place was amazing. They recreated a turn of the century town complete with old-fashioned signs, tin-plated roofing, gas lamps, cobblestone floors, etc. It was magnificent to see, and it was the talk of the town. I came up with a marketing slogan: "There's a new town in town!" And they both loved it. Greg never forgot my slogan and praised my "genius" to the skies. Genius, I ain't, but I enjoyed hearing him say it. Unfortunately, after a very strong opening, the place went totally downhill. Greg and Ed had a wonderful store that should have made millionaires out of them, but they put their trust in too many young employees, some of whom they'd pulled right off the street. Greg and Ed were such easygoing guys, and the employees robbed them blind. After just a couple of years, they threw in the towel. What a shame! It could have been one of the great Los Angeles attractions!

But that didn't stop Greg and me from hitting the local discos a couple of times a week. Those were the days. We would dance the night away, and on occasion I would wind up in bed with some cute guy. Compared to some friends, I was not promiscuous. I was never driven by sex, but I certainly did enjoy it. And compared to average guys in the straight life, I've probably had twenty times as many encounters as they've had. But I didn't go out every night, as so many friends had done. I'm very social, love to be with my friends, but I also love my down time. That's how it was then, and that's how it is now, except for the sex. There ain't any! Sex is grand, but it's not worth dying for.

Throughout the '70s I had a few short-lived affairs, three months or so. But I really didn't want another live-in arrangement. For the first time, I was on my own, and I was really enjoying my independence.

I managed to get a part-time job at Universal Studios, working on a made-for-TV film called *Testimony of Two Men*. The experience was a good one, and I hoped it might turn out to be a full-time job, but that never happened. However, it gave me the opportunity to work with Dan Dailey, whom I had always enjoyed, especially in his film musicals with Betty Grable. I interviewed him for the movie press book, and naturally, I brought up Grable. He told me that she was the funniest white lady he'd ever met. His exact words. He also said that when she was hospital-ized and near death, he wanted to see her, but she wouldn't permit it. She wouldn't see anyone, and those turned out to be her final days.

I also worked with Ralph Bellamy at his lovely home. He was a true old-school gentleman. I spent approximately two hours with him while he participated in a number of telephone interviews I had arranged. He was charming, and I loved how he called his wife "Mama."

After a few months, the job was over, and I was unemployed again. My friend Jack Lyons came to my rescue and managed to get me a job with a friend of his, a real sweet guy named Jerry Ballew. He owned his own typesetting shop, JB Typesets, in the San Fernando Valley, and I took to the trade quite easily. I found, in fact, that my work was incredibly accurate. I was highly dependable, and he always showed his appreciation. The job was going well, my boss was more like a buddy, and my social life was coming along in fine fashion. Then Max entered my life.

Max was a beautiful, young, godlike creature. The native-born Peruvian at one time dated my friend, Bud Greenberg, but they were no longer an item. He had lived in New York for years, but decided to give Los Angeles a whirl, and I was only too happy to temporarily share my one-bedroom (wink-wink) apartment with him. He arrived at LAX early in the morning, and I picked him up and drove him back to my place. It didn't take long for me to make my move. Max was a gorgeous young thing, and before you knew it, we were making sweet love. I felt a bit funny about it because of the Bud Greenberg connection, but they had severed their ties, although I knew that Max was carrying a big torch for him. Anyway, he stayed with me for approximately three months. We had sex regularly. I introduced him to my friends, and at the time, I thought

I was his one-and-only. But during one conversation with Max, it slipped out that he had gone to a notorious bathhouse that day, and from that time forward, things went rapidly downhill. After a while, I began to see through the young Adonis, and we didn't end the affair on a happy note. But it didn't take long to get over him. He wasn't the sweet young thing I thought he was.

Not long after that, my boss announced that he was closing up shop and moving to Arizona. I was very disappointed; I enjoyed the job. There was no one there to intimidate me, and Jerry had always been a fun guy to be with. Thanks to my typesetting background, I managed to land a job at Capitol Records in Hollywood. The year was 1980. I'll never forget my job interview. I was asked if I could get along with all types of people. I, of course, replied that I could. Then came the $64,000 question, "How about working for a tyrannical leader whom no one cared for?" I took a big gulp and told the man that I majored in psychology (liar, liar, pants on fire!), that I've handled many difficult types in the past and was sure that this would prove to be no different. And as it turned out, I was probably the only one in the printing department who actually got along well with Merv. He, in fact, invited me over to his home. I met his son, and we all had dinner out together. What can I say? When you got it, you got it! The problem with Merv was he had no tact. His marriage was falling apart; he was insecure and took his hard feelings out on the entire staff. All but me. I felt sorry for the guy. He was going through a divorce. He gave up a beautiful home, and he and his son since then lived together in a trailer. I too might have been testy under those conditions. Anyhow, he didn't last much longer in the department, and his job replacement turned out to be an extremely agreeable chap named Tommy Lazarus. He and I became very friendly. He was good-natured, fair-minded, and fun to be with. He was married with two kids, but he was a gay man who hadn't yet come out of the closet. I believe that was part of why he chose to become close to me. Not in a sexual way, but he enjoyed hearing about my life. He was also a huge Barbra Streisand fan, and I remember the two of us sneaking off one afternoon to see the movie *Yentl*. I felt very close to Tommy, and I developed friendships with a number of others in my department. It was a fun job that lasted eight years, and I would do it all over again in a heartbeat.

Every morning, a little old lady would accompany Takouhe ("Tako"), her physically impaired daughter, to work. Tako couldn't get around without a walker, but Mary, her mother seemed so fragile herself, I took pity on the elderly woman. I learned that Tako lived in the Hollywood area, not far from my home in West Hollywood, and wanting to be of help, I offered to pick Tako up each morning and take her home at night. This went on for a number of years until Mary had a terrible fall and wound up in a rest home. Tako, who was extremely dependent on her mom, was now on her own and the situation frazzled her right into a minor nervous breakdown. I visited Tako, who was now hospitalized, and then I went to see Mary. The rest home was just that - an actual home with a number of beds strewn about a sad, dark and dreary room. I'll never forget the look on Mary's face as I approached her bed. I'd never seen such a look of desperation. It was heartbreaking. She looked at me and pleaded for me to take her home. I tried to calm her down, but her pleading went on and on. I inquired about her condition with a staff member who told me that Mary was able to walk, but in order for her to be released it was imperative to obtain a doctor's okay. I told Mary, and her tears began to flow. "Please get me out of here now!" she cried. Once again, she began pleading. "I need to be with Tako," she shouted. My heart went out to her. I looked both ways. The attendant was nowhere to be seen. In a matter of seconds, I swooped Mary up in my arms, ran out the door with her, and before I knew it, the attendant was chasing after us. "You can't do that" she screamed. "Oh, yes I can," I screamed right back. Mary was now safely tucked away in my car, and in a short time, she was home and happy. Not long after the incident, Tako was herself again, and back with her mom. It may have been illegal taking Mary out like that, but I'm glad I did it.

My positive thinking helped in many respects, but some of the old bugaboos would crop up from time to time, and I was determined to overcome it. Shortly after being hired, I signed up for group therapy. The group consisted of approximately eight gay guys, all with different sorts of problems. It didn't really help me much to talk about my insecurities, but there was one guy in the group who was an absolute hunk. He obviously liked me too, and we shared one passionate evening together. Nothing serious. He really wasn't the settling-down kind of fella I was. In addition, and more importantly, I found a very good friend in Ron Friedman, a kind man who, unfortunately, suffered from very low self-esteem. But I liked him for his good heart, and we became close.

In 1980, my life was about to change in a big way. After having been on my own since the breakup with Joe, I was enjoying my freedom. And then I met Jerry Digney. I was out to dinner with Ron and a new friend named Lenny Williams, who, at one time, had been a clown at the Ringling Brothers circus. After dinner, we headed for a gay bar called Mickey's, and while we were there, we bumped into an old circus friend of Lenny's. Jerry had been the publicist for Ringling Brothers at one time, and at that time, he was working as a publicist for Circus Vargas. I didn't think all that much about him, but after a few drinks, I began to notice that Jerry was kind of sexy. I loved facial hair, and he had a nicely trimmed beard. We began to chat, and talking to him was easy because of our similar backgrounds in publicity. After an hour or so, we went to a corner bar called The Blue Parrot. The place was extremely full, and people were practically crushed together. I was feeling no pain by then, and I took full advantage of the situation and started to crush against Jerry. One thing, of course, led to another, and we were soon headed for his place in the hills, which was where he shared a home with famed circus owner, Clifford Vargas. I was impressed. The house had a 360 degree view of the city, which really was breathtaking. Vargas was out of town, and Jerry and I really clicked that evening on all levels. We traded numbers, which oftentimes leads nowhere fast, but I hoped he would call. After just a few days, he called, and the rest is history—twenty-three years' worth of history.

Chapter 8

COMPANY'S COMING

Dating Jerry was fun. He was extremely bright, ambitious, well-read, and he introduced me to the joys of motorcycle riding. Okay, I rode on the back, but it was fun hanging on! He was nice enough to surprise me with a pair of tickets to see Elton John at Dodger Stadium. However, the seats were in the very last row. I guess I had been spoiled by those years with Joe's upscale friends, and I sat there fuming and wondering if I had made a big mistake! Elton was no more than a speck. I got over it, of course, but just weeks later, an incident occurred which almost ended our relationship before it began. While brunching at a neighborhood café, I noticed a stream of hickeys across his neck. "We never agreed to be exclusive" was his story, but I was livid, so I did what any clear-minded thinker would do. I pushed the table over Jerry's chest, said a hasty good-bye, and meant it in more ways than one. That was it as far as I was concerned. We may not have called whatever we had exclusive, but when I'm intimate with someone, I expect the exclusivity part to be a non-issue. I can't really juggle myself from one person to another. It's just not who I am. A day or two later, while I was on the job at Capitol Records, a delivery boy came up to me, carrying a large balloon bouquet with a very sweet note of apology from Jerry. The gesture touched me, and I decided to give him another chance.

After a month or so of dating, Vargas moved from that lovely home in the hills to a condo in West Hollywood. Once again, Jerry was his roommate, and I saw him about twice a week. That was fine with me, since I had no intention of getting deeply involved. I'd lived alone for five years, and I was enjoying my independence. However, a few months into our relationship, he informed me that Vargas no longer wanted a roommate. He asked if he could stay with me temporarily until he found a place to live. Well, "temporarily" turned into twenty-three years. He moved in lock, stock, and barrel and didn't try very hard to seek other lodgings. Time went on, and eventually, it became official. Jerry and I were more than roomies. I was in love, and we were lovers. Considering the climate of the times, with

AIDS rearing its ugly head throughout the world, it was a good time to have a monogamous relationship. So what I originally thought might be an imposition on my single life turned out to be a blessing in disguise.

The first few years were very good. Jerry, for all his communication skill on the job, wasn't much of a communicator at home, but that was fine with me. I was pretty laid-back myself. The sex was good, and Jerry got along well with my friends, so I had no complaints. Things went smoothly for a while, but in time, I found that Jerry was not quite as thoughtful as I hoped he might be. I'm a bit of a romantic, and things like Valentine's Day are meaningful to me. Not for Jerry however. If I hadn't made a fuss, it would have been overlooked like any other day. I always saw to it that we celebrated at a good restaurant, but Jerry's indifference really bugged me. I sloughed it off a few times, but after a number of years, I grew tired of it, and we separated.

That was no time, however, to be footloose and fancy free. The black cloud of AIDS hung everywhere, and I, being the cautious type, did nothing of a sexual nature. I saw friends and spent time at home, which was fine with me. Jerry, on the other hand, moved to a building just next door and implied that he was back on the dating scene. Three months after our separation, I had a dinner party for friends, including Jerry. He stayed after everyone else left, and as I was cleaning up, he suggested that we get back together. He promised to be more thoughtful, and I decided to give it another try.

My job at Capitol Records was wonderful. I made friends, and nobody stood over me. I was practically my own boss, and my own boss, Tom, was a friend. I couldn't have asked for more. My social life with Jerry was good. Our circle of friends included Sham Haworth, Luis Monroe, Ed Bullard, Dick Roberts, and Lowell Mulligan; and I was happy as a clam. (How do we know that clams are happy, anyway?)

Ron, my new-found friend from group therapy, and Jerry were not at all compatible. In fact, Jerry found him to be annoying. Ron was a lonely guy, and I felt sorry for him; but if it was going to get in the way of my relationship with Jerry, I decided to keep my distance as well. Now, in hindsight, I never should have done it. I could have seen Ron and left Jerry to his own devices. It was a mistake, and I regret having done it.

One thing Jerry and I had in common was a desire to travel. A standout trip for me was the time we went to London, Paris, Venice, Milan, and Rome, and it was glorious. In London, we saw Al Pacino in the play, *American Buffalo*. He was outstanding, but it was September, and the theater had no air conditioning. It wasn't too comfortable, but Pacino's magnificent performance made it all worthwhile. In Paris, like the songs tell you, there was romance in the air. It was everything I had heard: charming and so conducive to romance. The food was expensive but sensational! The people, however, were not as friendly as I would have liked. I recall being in a department store and asking the clerk if she spoke English. She gave me a dirty look and gave me a harsh no. Later, I passed her by, and she was speaking broken English to a friend. I was thrilled at the sight of the Coliseum in Rome, the Vatican, the Fontana di Trevi; and the food, of course, was marvelous. We enjoyed lots of outdoor dining in lovely courtyards with twinkling lights overhead. It was all so romantic. Venice was charming. Riding in a gondola and perusing the many small shops along the narrow cobbled streets was a joy. Never had I felt so close to Jerry as I did during our European trip.

At that time, I decided to write a screenplay in the hope of reuniting the very successful screen team of Doris Day, Rock Hudson, and Tony Randall. The script was entitled *I Do/I Don't,* and the story revolved around a married couple (Doris and Rock) who, after twenty-some-odd years of marriage, decided to get a divorce. By then, Doris and I had communicated by letter for eight years. She had moved in 81, up north to the Carmel Valley, but our correspondence remained hot and heavy. Naturally, I sent my completed script to her, and I believe she really liked it. In fact, she explained in a letter to me that she wasn't just saying so because of our friendship. I also had sent a copy to Rock Hudson. He never replied, but during that period, I was invited to a birthday party, and who should be there? None other than Rock himself. I decided to have a little fun with him. I approached him very slowly, had a look on my face as if I was some crazed fan about to intrude on his space, and as I got closer, I slowly said, "Aren't you (long pause) Rex Stetson?" This was a character he portrayed in the motion picture, *Pillow Talk*. He laughed, and the ice was quickly broken. We chatted for a while, and during the course of our conversation, he mentioned that someone had written a follow-up to the highly successful comedy, *Pillow Talk*. He asked if I liked the title *Pillow Talk II*. I told him that it was far too long since the 1959 film had delighted moviegoers, and it wouldn't resonate with a young crowd of movie fans who'd never seen the original. He appreciated my opinion and seemed to agree. Jack Lyons, who was also there, told me a day or so later that after the party, he and a few others went to Rock's home, and Rock had mentioned that he was considering a few scripts designed to reunite him with Doris. One of those he mentioned was mine. It never happened, but I was thrilled nonetheless.

At this time, my ex-boss, Joe Fusco Jr., was starting his own production company back in New York. I sent him a copy of my screenplay, and much to my delight, he told me that he had read many scripts prior to mine, but mine stood out, and he wanted to produce it. I told him that I had Doris and Rock in mind, which didn't thrill him at all until his next visit to LA. I sat him down in front of the TV and played him a very recent interview of Doris on *Good Morning, America*, and he was instantly won over. "Oh yes, she's so right for it!" he declared. Of course, she was. With every word I wrote, I heard Doris's distinctive voice.

Joe began to set the wheels in motion. He sent a letter to Doris, expressing interest in having her star in the film. But she misunderstood and thought that he was referring to a TV series based on the script, and she declined. Shortly thereafter, he sent another letter, and even offered to meet her in Carmel or to hire a driver to pick her up and drive her to LA. We waited and waited for the reply that never came. It was obvious. Doris, by that time (1983), had no interest in resuming her show-business career. She had declined many good offers in the past and was heavily into her role as an animal rights advocate, which proved to be a labor of love. Sadly, one year later, Joe, who was only in his early forties, had a fatal heart attack. I miss him. He was a great, fun guy, and I adore his wife, Cheryl, whom I see to this day whenever I visit New York.

Jerry and I had a fairly active social life. Our friend, Ed Bullard, loved to entertain at home, and we enjoyed some wonderful dinners at his place. We also dined out frequently with him, Dick, Lowell, Sham, and his lover, Luis. I'll never forget one particular dinner at Ed's home. There were six of us at the table, including Jerry, when the subject of AIDS came up. Ed surprised us all by confessing that he had contracted the AIDS virus. I was shocked. Shortly after his proclamation, Sham Haworth stood up and told us the same sad tale about himself. As if that wasn't enough to absorb in one night, Lowell Mulligan popped up and told us the same terrible news. I found it extremely difficult to fall asleep that night. Two years later, they were all gone.

I remember sitting beside Ed as he lay on what was to become his deathbed. He looked like an Auschwitz victim. I felt so helpless as I sat there, trying to make pleasant conversation, which was not easy. I told him that he just might defy the odds. Nobody really knows his body and how it might respond to treatment. That's what I told him, but I didn't really believe it.

Lowell was a funny guy, not in a bad way, but in a ha-ha, funny way. He loved to tell jokes, and he relished being in the spotlight. His final days were so sad. He spent those days in hospice care and was no longer able to communicate, which must have felt like a term in solitary prison for that one-time life of the party.

Sham was simply the sweetest, most thoughtful guy on the planet, and his loss was felt deeply by anyone who was lucky enough to have known him.

Chapter 9

POSITIVE CHANGE

In 1987, I attended a Doris Day convention in Carmel, California. Approximately fifty or sixty of us fans got together, and thanks to Mike Doyle, who headed a collector's club, Doris attended the affair. When she entered the hotel hall, she took our collective breaths away. There she was, our idol, looking stunning, years younger than her age (which was sixty-five at the time) and being totally gracious to our group. We gave her a standing ovation, and in typically modest Doris Day style, she motioned for us to stop and to sit down. First, we had a buffet lunch, then a Q and A session with Doris, which must have lasted for at least two hours. Later, she gave each of us a little one-on-one time, and a photographer took our individual pictures with her. It was quite an afternoon.

Not long after that, I lost my job at Capitol Records. My boss was going through a really traumatic time, and unfortunately, his trauma affected my life and the lives of others in the department as well. Tommy was a closet homosexual, and his marriage was falling apart. His daughter was constantly running away from home, he was having an affair with a very young guy in our office, and he decided to go into a mail-order business selling men's underwear. On the premises and after hours, he took pictures of young, well-built guys and elected me to help put the catalogue together with my typesetting skills. I didn't want to become involved, but what choice did I have? He was my boss. Somehow, word got out over at the Capitol Tower, which housed the executives, and before long, we were out on our asses. That was a hard blow because I felt right at home on that wonderful job.

It took me quite a while to find another job, but I eventually landed a typesetting gig at the Electro Ad Agency, an in-house agency for the Hewlett-Packard Co. It wasn't bad, and the pay was good, but the trip was quite a distance from home. Battling the notorious LA traffic each day was exasperating. Additionally, typesetting was on the way out; personal computers were quickly taking over. Magazines and newspapers were using them, and I could see the writing on the wall. But I carried on for a while.

One unforgettable day, I got a call at work from my brother, Phil. Dad had died. I walked back to my office space, didn't tell a soul, and began to cry softly to myself. And then a thought occurred to me. On the last day of my last visit to New York, I called Mom and Dad to say good-bye, and Dad said something completely out of character. He asked me if I could come back to see him just one more time before I go. I had already made plans for my final evening, so I told him I would see him again next time around. I believe he had a premonition that my last visit would be just that, my last visit, and it was.

Later that day, I told my boss, Tom, that I'd be heading back to the Bronx in the morning for my father's funeral. He understood, and when I got back home, there was a gorgeous flower arrangement sent by the company to me and my family. I stayed in New York for a week or so and, on the way back to California, decided it was time to find a new job.

The salary at Electro Ad was okay, but I thought I could do better. I made the mistake of sharing my feelings with a fellow worker, and the word obviously got out. Tom called me into his office and asked me how much of a raise would induce me to stay. I was flabbergasted. I'd never received such a generous offer. I made my bid, and he accepted without hesitation. I wasn't sure it would happen, but sure enough, I was given the raise, and I sent Tom a card, telling him that he's a man of his word and that I was truly grateful. I stayed on for a while, but there was that long drive to contend with, and it was getting tiresome.

Onward and upward, I found a new job closer to home at a local typesetting house. The variety of work held new challenges. My boss was an affable Irishman who loved to tell the blarney, and I worked with two gals, a fellow type-setter and a graphic artist. But once again, my old fears reared their ugly head, and for no reason at all, one of the gals simply spooked me, just the old psychobabble coming back to haunt me. It became so bothersome, that before long, I was back in therapy. My therapist was an attractive middle-aged lady named Sandy, and we had a nice rapport. There were times, in fact, when I felt a physical attraction to her, but that I kept at bay. She was quite good, and I found my self-confidence becoming stronger with each session. Looking back at the three therapists I've had in my life, I'd say that my sessions with Sandy were the most productive.

Things began to fall apart in '91. For some reason, Jerry no longer was interested in joining me for dinners out with our friends. After a while, I grew very tired of having to make excuses for his many absences. Additionally, after eleven years, sex just wasn't the same. We were bored. One evening, while preparing to leave for dinner with the guys, I decided to put Jerry to the test. I asked him to please come along. Then I added that it would mean so much to me if he came. He wouldn't budge. I went out without him but was determined to put an end to our relationship. A good relationship shouldn't have to be a strain, and at that point, a strain it was.

When I'm full of emotion and need to make an important point, I do much better in a letter than in a one-on-one conversation. That way, my emotions don't get in the way of clear thinking, and I can't be interrupted. And so I left a letter for Jerry the next morning. It stated in no uncertain terms that our relationship was over, and that I hoped we could remain friends. And thankfully, we have done so. That evening, we had a short discussion, but it was what it was. I wasn't about to change my mind. Jerry tried making the moves on me in bed that night, but I made it clear that I meant business. Before too long, he was sleeping in our guest room.

Funny, in business, Jerry is a tower of strength, but when it came to his personal life, he really needed a significant someone by his side. After eleven years of being lovers, I was mourning the end of a long-time relationship, but Jerry was not. He began going out just about every night. I warned him time after time that he was playing with fire, but he wasn't about to listen. During that trying period I also lost my job. I remained under the same roof with Jerry, but it was rough going. I had no idea what the future held. I needed a positive change in my life. Introducing Jack Hewson.

I had met Jack a year or so prior to my breakup with Jerry. We met at a New Year's Eve party that Jerry and I had thrown at our home. Our friends had brought him along, and I found him to be a delightful gent. He loved our place, called the décor, "New York style," and this ex-New Yorker couldn't have received a nicer compliment.

Jack was an older man, seventy-three or so. He had no family, and he couldn't really get around much because he had given up driving years earlier. I decided to call him to, hopefully, make a new friend. We began going to dinner once or twice a week, and afterward, we'd usually stop at Gelson's so he could do his shopping. In time, we became close, and he began to depend on me. We enjoyed each other's company, and in our own way, we were important to one another.

After quite some time, I finally landed a job with a newspaper that was run by an absolute tyrant. I liked the work, however, because the people in the office were nice, and I made new friends. The downside was the owner, who worked us to the bone. Oftentimes I would work a sixteen-hour day, and I'd never receive overtime. I was not the only victim of his stingy ways. Others worked equally hard, and none of us fought back because we all needed the work.

After about a year on the job, the company moved to Beverly Hills, and before long, the tightwad began to cut my work schedule down. I was now working three days a week, but sometimes, my days were about sixteen hours long! I didn't mind because I enjoyed the work and the people, but not getting overtime really grated on my nerves! I'd had enough of it. I decided to look around for another job, and after a while, I found it at Heritage Publications. That too, was a part-time, three-day-a-week job, but I no longer had to put up with a tyrant.

Heritage was a newspaper with appeal to the Jewish community. Upon entering the premises, I saw a guy with a long beard, and the first thing that came to mind was that it was a religious organization. I couldn't have been more mistaken. As it turned out, the guy with the beard was a film extra who specialized in portraying homeless bums. And to give you an idea as to how religious it was, the place was open on Saturdays (Shabbat), a no-no in Jewish tradition. I was scheduled to work Sunday through Tuesday, and that worked out fine for me.

In the meantime, Jerry had linked up with a young Asian boy named Jimmy Lam. Thankfully, Jerry's wandering ways had come to an end. The relationship lasted about two years, and there we were, Jerry, Jimmy, me, and their new dog, Maya. Charly, my cat, evidently enjoyed the new addition, especially when he was being humped by Ms. Maya. She was no lady!

I was still friendly with Robie and a new friend, a fellow Bronxite named Betty Rogers whom Karen had introduced me to. And since Jerry and I were leading separate lives, I rekindled my friendship with Ron.

I'm not a big believer in astrology, but if what they say about Virgos is correct, we like things in their proper place, and that fits me to a *t*. All of a sudden, Jerry became a real hoarder of books, and there were piles everywhere. For a while, I buttoned my lip and had to step begrudgingly over piles of books. But eventually, it got to me, and I threatened to go my own way if he didn't clean up his act. He did, and things went smoothly for a while.

Jerry and Jimmy broke up after two years or so, and Jerry was out and about again. I went for a mini-vacation to Florida to visit my cousins, Betty and her husband Sid, two people I adore. While there, I also saw my ex, Joe, and all in all, the three days spent there were great. I'm so grateful to have Betty and Sid, such wonderful cousins, and it was great to see Joe again.

Chapter 10

HELLO DORIS, GOODBYE JACK

Jack and I would go out to dinner twice a week on average. We frequented one place in particular, an unpretentious neighborhood restaurant called The Silver Spoon. A number of local celebrities were often seen there, as well as the local regulars, enjoying the down-to-earth fare. I saw Shelley Winters, Robert Forster, and Doris Roberts there a number of times. The food wasn't great, but the people-watching was fun.

Working at Heritage was a walk in the park. I didn't feel threatened by anyone, and it was a joy to simply relax, do my job, and go home. At work, we were all friends, and although the owners knew nothing about running a business, we employees enjoyed the relaxed atmosphere. I see a number of my coworkers to this day.

I was still skittish about having a sexual relationship. I enjoy sex as much as anyone, but with the dark cloud of AIDS hanging over our gay little heads, my penis head, I felt, should best be left behind my fly.

After roughly a year of abstinence, I dated a guy about my age. He was not only a cutie, but he had a body to die for. He lived in Glendale, which was only a twenty-minute drive from home, and we dated for a while; but unfortunately, he just wasn't that into me! So we never sealed the deal.

Sometime later, I met a much younger guy, who was an orchestra conductor and a big honcho at the Orange County Performing Arts Center. He was a looker, and one evening, he invited me to a performance of *Pacific Overtures,* a Stephen Sondheim musical that is rarely seen anywhere. I enjoyed the show, particularly watching my new friend conduct the orchestra. After the show, we went to his place, which was beautiful. We played some Scrabble (yeah, we really did!). And later, I'd like to say that the conductor and I made beautiful music together, but sex with him was unsettling. He was into getting large sex toys shoved up his butt, and right then and there, I knew that would be my last trip to the OC. After just one night, he asked me to move to Orange County. One night! I never saw him again.

One day, Jack asked if I would be willing to visit his friend, Ralph Zeek, once a week to help him with chores.

Ralph suffered from macular degeneration, and I wound up seeing him every Wednesday to help with marketing, banking, or whatever. He enjoyed giving me massages—strictly legit—and paid me $20 for each visit, which lasted two to three hours. Since I was only working part-time, the twenty bucks came in handy. But after a month or so, I told him to keep his money. We became fast friends, and I just felt funny taking the dough from him. But I did look forward to Wednesdays with Ralph because he was a sweet man with an outgoing personality. One thing was a constant: he would save a week's worth of *The Los Angeles Times* and wanted me to read him the obituaries. "Just want to check and see if I'm still alive," he'd joke. Ralph was in his late seventies; I suppose he wanted to see the ages of those who had passed on. But we had lots of laughs together, and he was a good storyteller. At one time, Ralph was a contract player at MGM, and between his background and mine in showbiz publicity, we enjoyed sharing our past experiences. After a couple of months, Ralph's massaging hands were creeping down into uncharted territory. I kept pushing those insistent fingers away, but after a few months of fighting it, I decided to see where it goes. As it turned out, he wanted to give me oral sex, and after being celibate all those many years, I asked myself, "Why not?" That went on for a couple of years until the sad time when Ralph passed away. I'll always have fond memories of our times together.

The years flew by quickly, as they tend to do the older one gets. Jerry met his current lover David Marshall, and in no time flat, he was living in our home. I was a bit resentful, not because of David, but Jerry gave me no indication that that kid was moving in. I just turned around, and there he was. Welcome to my world!

In 1998, I received a call from a young man named Pierre Patrick. He told me there was a Doris Day musical tribute show about to open at the brand-new Falcon Theatre in Burbank, California. Famed producer Gary Marshall owned that beautiful venue. Pierre had heard that I had a collection of Doris Day posters and asked if I'd be willing to lend them out to decorate the theatre's interior. I was only too happy to do this. During that period, Pierre and I became friendly, and a short time later, since he didn't drive, he asked if I would drive him and actress Jackie Joseph up to Carmel to meet with Doris. *Would* I? Talk about a no-brainer! Jackie was a regular on the CBS-TV sitcom *The Doris Day Show,* and she was a delight to be with, just a very sweet, down-to-earth lady.

Anyway, as it turned out, we joined Doris's friend, Bill Glynn, to meet with Doris for lunch at the Quail Lodge. Doris was seventy-five at the time, and she looked a good fifteen years younger. I was delighted to see her looking so well, and she sat right beside me as we dined with the others in our group. I couldn't contain my joy and turned to Doris and said, "I'm so happy to be here!" She turned to me and, in true-to-form modesty, replied, "I like this place too." Later that evening, Jackie told me that Doris had said to her, "How about that Howard? Sweeet!" That was wonderful to hear, and it was so good of Jackie to tell me.

Two days later, we joined Doris once again, that time for brunch. After a nice meal, we were invited to spend time in her home, and like the lady herself, it was attractive and unpretentious, not at all what you'd expect to see in the home of the number 1 female box-office star in movie history. There was not a sign of the many awards, nominations, and gold records she'd received over the course of an amazing three-decade career. It was quite a weekend!

By then, Jack, who was pushing eighty-five, was beginning to have some health problems. He was losing his balance, so I bought him a cane. He used it for a while, and it seemed to help. But one evening, I will never forget. Jack asked me to stand up; he rested his hands on my shoulder and tried to walk from behind me. He couldn't do it, and he fell back on the couch. I realized that he was going to need help on a daily basis. I quit my volunteer deliveries for Meals on Wheels and Project Angel Food and came to visit Jack every day. I usually spent about half a day with him. I bought his groceries, microwaved his lunches and dinners, and out of necessity, brought him a bedpan, which I cleaned out each morning. It was tough going, but Jack had been good to me, I appreciated it, and this was the least I could do. My daily schedule since then revolved around him.

His condition worsened with time, and he found it difficult to eat. I tried everything—all his favorite foods—but to no avail. He was going downhill fast. I kept telling him he needed to see a doctor, but Jack, who never saw doctors, resisted mightily for quite some time. I felt helpless as I watched my friend deteriorate more and more with each long, passing day. Finally, I asked him, "Jack, what can I do to help?" He started to bang away furiously at his head and shouted "Kill me! Kill me!" He meant business, but I wasn't about to do away with my pal. One morning, he said, "Take me to the hospital." Boy, for him to make such a request, he had to be feeling terrible. I called for an ambulance, and in no time, he was in the emergency room at Cedars-Sinai hospital in Los Angeles. The room was cold and crowded, and the catheter they stuck in his penis didn't help matters. He screamed up a storm until they couldn't stand it anymore, and it was removed. As weak as he was, he still had a powerful pair of lungs. Then we waited and waited and waited some more. Rooms were not available, and after a very long five-hour stretch in this cold corridor, Jack got his room at last.

I visited him daily. Jack was not an easy patient; he grumbled to me, grumbled to the staff, and they couldn't wait, I'm sure, to see him go. On one particular visit, there was a sign on his door to enter with a mask. Huh? I put the mask on, but that didn't last very long. I think the staff thought he might have AIDS, but that was not only impossible, it was ridiculous. After a week or so, the nurses lightened their load and sent Jack to a rest home on Melrose Avenue in Hollywood. He didn't fare any better there. They tried getting him on his feet to walk, but that wasn't going to happen. He still wasn't eating at that point, and after five days or so, they shipped him off to Century City Hospital. Once again, he was irritable to the staff, and when they suggested inserting a tube into his stomach to get some nutrition in him, he bellowed, "If you dare, I'll sue the hell out of you!" The doctors tried to talk me into convincing him, but I knew Jack. I tried to talk some sense into him, but he resisted strongly, so I didn't bother to make any further attempts.

He was sent home not long after that, and as soon as he landed on the couch, he asked for a cigarette. Under normal circumstances, I wouldn't have given him one, but if one cigarette would make him feel just a little better, I decided to grant him his wish. He took a few puffs, and then the cigarette fell to the floor. I wasn't about to let him and his house go up in smoke when I wasn't around, so I grabbed the cigarette and told him that he was no longer a smoker. He didn't argue, and that was that.

The next morning, which was appropriately gray and rainy, I entered his home to find him in a state of rigor mortis. It was inevitable. He had hardly eaten for a couple of months. I had put a quick stop to his smoking, and I'm sure his will to live had been at an all-time low. Still, I was shocked; but after regaining my composure, I looked him straight in his open eyes and screamed, "Jack, your night-mare is over!" I was actually happy for him. I called 911, and soon, a couple of police officers showed up. Shortly after, the morticians arrived, holding that ominous black bag in which Jack was about to leave the home he loved. It was a sad moment indeed. Jack was a good friend, and we really enjoyed each other's company. But he was ready to go. There was no diagnosed illness. I believe his body simply gave out.

Jack had asked me to be the administrator of his estate. He kept his will in a metal file box, and when I took a peek, I was astonished to find that he had left me his home, plus $100,000 after estate taxes had been settled. Wow. I had always done well financially, but that kind of money was new to me. He changed my life. But first, there was the business of settling his business.

Jack owned a duplex in Los Angeles. A fellow named Dick Robison had lived in the adjoining unit for thirty years or so, and it was up to me to break the news that I would be selling the house. I would have occupied it myself if it had been in good condition, but that was hardly the case. So I was left to do the dirty work. I called Dick, gave him sufficient time to move out and, hopefully, settle in the Laguna Niguel condo he had owned for many years. Not quite as easy as it sounds. Dick resisted mightily, and even though I gave him six months, he was not about to give up the ship. I understood his feelings. He was elderly; he loved his home, and the thought of moving, I'm sure, was not something he had envisioned at that stage of his life. But I needed to sell the house, and after six months, I put it on the market. It didn't take long for a prospective buyer to show interest. I told Dick and gave him two more months in which to make the move. He fought me like a tiger and just wouldn't give in. He did his homework and found that it would have been illegal to evict him, and eventually, I lost the sale. Time went on; and finally, after about a year, Dick had a change of heart and informed me that he was ready to move on. The house went back on the market, and before long, it was sold.

After I consulted with a financial advisor and had a few dollars in the bank, I was ready to find my own place. As luck would have it, a townhouse in my complex, similar to the one I'd shared with Jerry, opened up, and I grabbed it. I'd never given decorating a serious thought, but I wanted that place to be my little piece of paradise and went into decorating with gusto. To my surprise, I enjoyed it immensely, and judging by the comments I've received, I must have been pretty good at it. The house turned out just as I'd envisioned it, and Charly and I were two happy campers living there. If I had known, back when I was about seventeen, what fun decorating could be, I would have pursued it as a career. I bought a special designer box in which to house Jack's ashes; it's a beautiful box and was the least I could do for a man who changed my life in the best of ways.

After the dust settled, I decided to go on a bit of a spree. Why not? I was a millionaire, if only for a few years. Couldn't hold onto that lofty title for too long since I had no pension, and my investments were drawing very little interest. But I wanted just a taste of the high life. For my next trip back east, I stayed at the luxurious Four Seasons Hotel. I liked it so much that I stayed there another three times. After a few years, my finances dwindled a bit, so I downscaled in a small way and stayed at the Essex House on Central Park West, another great hotel. That was the extent of my extravagance.

Charly acclimated easily to the new digs. He was a great cat—more like a puppy dog than a feline. He'd follow me everywhere, and he usually met me at the door when I arrived home. But I began to notice that he was losing weight. I tried everything to make him well, took him to the vet then to another vet who made house calls and then to a specialist, but it looked like the end of the line for my best friend. Finally, I was forced to put him down. He was over twenty, and he had a good life, so that was a bit of a consolation, but knowing that was never quite good enough. I missed my fuzzy little friend.

Every Friday night, I would go out to dinner with my cousins Karen and her hubby, David, two of the dearest people on Earth. Once in a while, Lisa and Moshe Eitani, another married couple, would join us. Lisa was a delight, fun to be with. But her husband was the total opposite. He had a grouchy demeanor and was not very willing to extend himself. Speaking to Lisa about Moshe made it obvious to me that she wasn't thrilled with him either. Not long after I met them, she filed for divorce.

Chapter 11

A HAPPY ENDING

My friend Betty lived in Pasadena, just a half-hour drive from home. I didn't mind the trip because driving provided me with one of my greatest pleasures: I love singing along with the radio. It just makes me happy. We had some wonderful times sampling the array of great restaurants in old town Pasadena. We both loved good food, and we always had plenty to talk about. Every now and then, we'd take in a movie. We cried like babies when we saw *Babe,* the popular film about a farmer and his pig. We had to laugh about that, but the movie was quite touching, and I know many who were similarly affected. But after all the good times we shared, Betty cut me out of her life just like that. I made plans with her for dinner one Sunday evening, but I'd forgotten that it was the

Sunday I had committed to my aunt Joan and uncle Irving. I called Betty and asked if we could reschedule for the following evening. She ended the call abruptly, and next thing I knew, she sent me an e-mail cutting me totally out of her life. Was she looking for an excuse? Who knows? She never gave me the benefit of hearing her out, and she left me with not a bit of closure. Not nice at all. I thought our friendship went deeper than that.

She's not the only long-time friend to just suddenly drop out of my life. Years before the Betty episode, Robie, whom I had known for twenty years, did the same. In 1995, my cat had somehow gotten out of the house. Upon discovery, I made up signs to post throughout the neighborhood, and I called Robie to tell him of my plight. He didn't sound at all concerned for me (or Charly), and I was disappointed in that he didn't offer to help. Thankfully, a short time later, a neighbor rang my bell to inform me that he found Charly hiding beneath a nearby car. I dashed to the car, called out Charly's name, and he came running to me. I was still a bit upset about Robie's couldn't-care-less attitude. I decided to wait for his call. It's now over twenty years, and I'm still waiting! I sent him a card and asked what has happened to the friendship I had once valued? He never answered. How those two supposedly good friends could simply turn me off is puzzling. Losing their friendship is one thing, but not getting closure is a bitch.

Although retired, I kept busy. I delivered for Meals on Wheels a couple of days a week, and for Project Angel Food as well. I saw my friend Ron three times a week, had dinner with Karen and David every Friday night, saw Lisa from time to time, and my life was full.

Mother passed away in 1997, but I've continued to go back to New York as often as I can. After all these years away, it still feels like home. There really is no place like New York City. I enjoy the hustle and bustle. Even when nothing is happening, you can feel excitement in the air. It's great seeing old friends, my brother and niece, cousins Betty and Sid, and the theatre. We have theatre in LA, but it just can't compare with the thrill of a Broadway show! I can't think of a better vacation.

Two of my long-time New York friends are Paul Langer and his wife, Fran. I hadn't seen them in about forty years, not since I left Helene and left them with no explanation as to why I was gone. I thought about them from time to time and wondered how they were doing. Well, I subscribed to a website called Classmates.com. I didn't really expect to link up immediately with Paul, but as luck would have it, he was listed as a member. I sent him an e-mail, and before I knew it, he replied with a "Wow, I've been trying to find you for so long!" On my next visit back east, we reunited, and it was just like old times. I continued to see him and Fran each time I went back until they moved to Florida, and now, unfortunately, I don't get that chance. But we do stay in touch.

On one recent visit, I rang up Helene, long remarried and living in Connecticut and asked if we could get together for dinner. I was so happy when she accepted my invitation, and we had a lovely time together just catching up on our lives. I was glad to hear how happy she is, and she seemed as glad to see me as I was to see her. Most importantly, I got the chance to let her know that when we were married, I was honestly in love with her.

I subscribed to a newspaper called *The Pelham Parkway Times,* a publication for us old Bronxites, and I enjoyed the nostalgic stories, photos, and articles written by familiar names, and some who were not so familiar. I even contributed a story about Doris and me. I really got a kick out of this paper and called the publisher to tell him so. During the course of our conversation, he mentioned that Mel Citrin was trying to find me. Mel Citrin! Now there was a welcome name from out of my past. I hung out with him back in the '50s. I couldn't wait to find out how he was doing. I called him, and we had a wonderful conversation about old times. As it turned out, he was married to his college sweetheart, a gal named Phyllis. I arranged to meet him the next time I hit New York, and we met the following May. We dined at a fancy midtown restaurant and had a great time. He may have been older, but he was quite young at heart, and he dressed and groomed himself like a guy half his age. Most older guys who try to dress inappropriately young look silly, but on Mel, it looked good! We share a love for the theatre and made a vow to attend a show together every time I came to town. On subsequent visits, I met his wife, Phyllis, an extremely intelligent and fun gal, and it's always great being in their company.

By then I was growing tired of my friendship with Ron. He didn't have many other friends, so he became heavily dependent on me and took up a great deal of my time, so much so that I really had little time to cultivate new friendships. More importantly, he had little respect for my feelings, and his insensitivity made my nerves rise to a boiling point on more than one occasion. Many times, he would turn to me and say, "You're not going to like what I'm about to say." I, in turn, would say, "Well, then don't say it!" But he always managed to spit it out, and after twenty or so years of that verbal abuse, I finally decided to put an end to it! After one particularly unpleasant dinner out, I rushed home, determined to sever my ties with him once and for all. I headed straight to the keyboard on which I'm typing this memoir and told him in no uncertain terms what I should have said long ago. I made it clear that I was no longer going to be verbally abused, and our friendship was over. Case closed.

He called me shortly after receiving the e-mail, but I didn't pick up the phone. The message he left indicated his sorrow and a promise to be more respectful in the future. Back to the keyboard, I went. We'd been down that road before, and his short-term good behavior never lasted long. It was over, and I truly hoped that someday he'd find a way to release the anger inside that has hounded him for a lifetime.

I've been a loyal reader of show business columnist Liz Smith since I was a child. In 2005, she included an item that piqued my interest. She wrote that David Kaufman was preparing a biography of Doris Day that promises to give the lady her due as an actress and singer and reveal what went on behind the shiny blonde facade.

Ms. Day's reputation as a singer and actress was badly smeared during the sexual revolution of the late '60s. I grew so tired of hearing her mistakenly referred to as the perpetual virgin that I drafted a letter, which I sent out to any media people who propagated that unfortunate label.

Comedienne Joy Behar recently made that mistake on the television show, *The View*, and I had to send her the following letter:

I was delighted to hear on yesterday's show that you, like I and millions of others, are a Doris Day fan. However, it really is time that people discontinued to propagate the myth that DD portrayed virgins. It's just not true. For the most part, Ms. Day was an independent, successful career woman who was as interested in love and all that goes with it as any red-blooded American girl would be. She just didn't want to hop in the sack with anyone for a one-night stand. That doesn't a virgin make. It simply depicts a woman with principles. Additionally, she portrayed mothers in 25 percent of her films. Try doing that as a virgin!

I don't know if she ever received my letter, but hopefully, she did and won't add to the unfortunate myth any longer.

I felt obligated to get in touch with author David Kaufman because I too wanted desperately to see Ms. Day take her proper place in the history of film and records. After all these years of following her and her career, I've become something of a Doris Day historian, and I wanted to advise him as to people he might not have considered for interviews. And so, I e-mailed Liz Smith, asking to have Kaufman get in touch with me, and in short time, he called. I arranged to meet him on my next trip to New York. And for the next three years, I advised him, encouraged him, and in 2008 when the book was finally published, I suggested some ideas for publicity that turned out to get him some wonderful media exposure. The book, entitled, *Doris Day, The Untold Story of the Girl Next Door*, was a resounding success and became a *New York Times* best seller. I was very happy to be a part of the project and was pleasantly surprised when David included a photo of me and Doris in the book. I believe it is the definitive biography to date, and I'm proud to have taken part in it.

Now that Ron was out of my life, I was determined to make new friends. I read about a senior gay group called Project Rainbow, which was held every Wednesday for a one-hour social period at Plummer Park in West Hollywood. Joining that was one of the best decisions I ever made. I've made wonderful new friends, and my social life has never been better. I continue to do volunteer work twice a week for Meals on Wheels, and it does my heart good to make a contribution, no matter how small, to the community.

As I look back on growing up in one of the top dysfunctional families of all time—a mother with a serious mental problem, a father who verbally and physically abused me, kids who tormented me with their relentless teasing—I've got to give myself credit as I've come out of the abyss relatively unscathed. Despite years of anxiety, fleeing from people, and bowing out of great job opportunities, I'm still here, and I'm happier than I've ever been! Sure, I've still got a few scars, but when all is said and done, they haven't gotten me!

About the Author

Howard Green resides in North Hollywood, California. Born in the Bronx to as-dysfunctional-as-they-get parents, he had many emotional hurdles to overcome over the course of his lifetime, and conquer he did through perseverance, meditation, and a host of psychiatrists. Working for some top motion picture studios, he found himself mixing with the likes of Jack Lemmon, Clint Eastwood, Lucille Ball, John Denver, and the list goes on and on.

Fixated on singer-actress Doris Day since childhood, he went from an over-the-top fan to a friend, and he has shared some many memorable moments with the star. Now retired, his pastimes today include theatre-going, music appreciation, travel, and volunteer work. Most of all, he has a strong desire to spread loving vibrations to friends, acquaintances, particularly to those in need of a sympathetic ear. Being Green was a long time in the making and was not originally intended to become a published work. However, after the insistence of friends, who hung on to every word of his story it is here to be enjoyed, and hopefully, to be an inspiration to those who feel there is no light at the end of the tunnel.